'A compendium of good advice from her *Sunday Times* columns, *Dear Dolly* is Dolly Alderton at her wise, warm and witty best. All of human life is contained in these pages: from dating apps to eating disorders, too much sex, not enough sex and the ebb and flow of friendships, relationships and situationships. I felt like a better, kinder person for having read these letters and Dolly's thoughtful replies' *Red*

'Her refreshing take makes for compulsive reading. The result is an oddly soothing book, as the problems of others leave you not with a sense of schadenfreude but with the comforting realization that something you have felt, or are feeling, has been felt by countless others – and it will always be that way' *Daily Mail*

'With a thoughtful essay about what answering others' questions has taught her, this collection of Alderton's agony aunt advice offers bundles of empathy (and zero judgement) about life's problems, from totally relatable dilemmas to the entertainingly voyeuristic' *Grazia*

'Capturing the hearts and minds of young romantics and dreamers, she offers sage and sisterly advice to those in need' Magic Radio Book Club

'Alderton's wise words can resonate with women of all ages. She feels like a best friend and your older sister all rolled into one and her pages wrap around you like a warm hug' *Evening Standard*, on *Everything I Know About Love*

'Alderton has struck a chord with a generation . . . Invaluable . . . A must for diehard Dolly fans' *Heat*

'Dolly Alderton is so gifted at making people care. A rare talent' Marian Keyes

'Alderton is Nora Ephron for the millennial generation' Elizabeth Day

'Dolly Alderton is never less than dazzling on the travails of the human heart' Clover Stroud

Dear Dolly

ABOUT THE AUTHOR

Dolly Alderton is an award-winning author, screenwriter and journalist based in London. She is a columnist for *Sunday Times Style* and has also written for *GQ*, *Red*, *Marie Claire* and *Grazia*. She is the former co-host and co-creator of the podcast *The High Low*. Her first book, *Everything I Know About Love*, became a top-five *Sunday Times* bestseller in its first week of publication, won a National Book Award for Autobiography of the Year and was made into a BBC One TV series. *Ghosts,* her first novel, was published by Fig Tree in 2020.

For India Masters, my agony aunt.

Contents

Introduction   ix

Dating   1
Friendship   35
Relationships   69
Family   111
Sex   129
Break-ups & Exes   159
Body & Soul   189

Acknowledgements   215
Bonus Columns   217

Introduction

I was at an all-time low when I decided I wanted to try to fix everyone else's problems. My head was a mess and my heart was broken. It was one of those years where every month brought a new sadness – an *annus horribilis*, I think they call it. And, in a mean-spirited move from Fate, My Bad Year also coincided with THE Bad Year – 2020. The most *horribilis* of all the *annuses*.

During that time, I pitched myself as an agony aunt to my editor at the *Sunday Times Style*. In my twenties, I had written a weekly dating column for the magazine, a fact that occasionally knocks down the door of my sub-conscious in the middle of the night and wakes me up in a cold sweat. But it remains one of the best job opportunities I have ever been given. And 26 to 28 years old is the perfect time for a person to comfortably narrate their own life for entertainment. It is the sweet spot of exhibitionism, where your lack of self-awareness makes for main-character-syndrome capers, counterbalanced with JUST enough self-awareness to make jokes about them. I finished the column, wrote a memoir about my twenties, then closed up shop for the serialization of my personal life. I'd finally shared enough.

This briefly left me in a journalistic no-man's-land.

Having written a memoir, people wanted me to continue to insert myself in stories, even when my presence was completely irrelevant to the subject matter. Editors would commission me to write about people, places and things under the pretence of being a neutral observer, then inevitably ask me to crowbar references to my personal life into the copy. During this time, I could have interviewed Barack Obama, and I would have seen: 'PERHAPS YOU COULD WRITE HERE ABOUT HOW YOUR STORY IS SIMILAR TO HIS?? DOES YOUR DATING LIFE HAVE ANY PARALLELS WITH HIS TIME IN OFFICE?? DOES HE REMIND YOU OF AN EX-BOYFRIEND ETC??' in the notes from any editor.

Which, of course, I understood. I was the one who had insisted on telling everyone about my life, no one had asked that of me in the first instance. I did try to write a first-person column that included hardly any present-day detail about my life in any intimate way. But the thing that makes a first-person column interesting is the admission of the writer's flaws, mistakes and disasters, so this was challenging, to say the least. I was also not an opinion columnist. My skin is too thin, my mind too changeable and my courage too paltry. So, with no personal life or public opinions for material, this left me with very little to write about, other than general enthusiastic musings about things I liked. Or mealy-mouthed non-rants about things I didn't like, cushioned with self-conscious caveats. One of my friends called this sort of gentle, forgettable column-writing: 'I Changed the Batteries in my Remote Control' journalism. I did not want this to become my legacy.

But I had always wanted to be an agony aunt. In my adolescence, I would buy teen magazines and immediately skip to the problem pages. Sex was discussed in my house, I imagine much more than it would have been for boomers (the last victims of Victorian parenting). But there were no specifics. Instead, it was couched in the vagaries of baby-making and 'tingly feelings' and 'when you care about someone very much'. This was not enough for me. I needed more. Problem pages were my salvation – my perverted eyes would dart over the pages looking for key words: 'virginity', 'masturbation', 'discharge'. I took these tips and passed them off as my own, becoming the Playground Sexual Yoda. I would vastly exaggerate my own experiences and give counsel to girls my own age and older.

One of my biggest regrets is that I found childhood and adolescence such a humiliating place to be. When I read my teenage diaries now, I recognize how much I was lying to the page because I was so embarrassed about how young I was. I speak wearily of sex, like I'm bored of it, when I hadn't even been touched. I note the number of calories and cigarettes I consumed that day, like a jaded divorcee. I wished away my life, unaware I was the proprietor of a material more valuable than gold: youth. I wanted no part in it for my entire childhood. I think my obsession with being an agony aunt perhaps stemmed from this desire – I wanted to be the well-lived woman handing out advice, rather than the galumphing schoolgirl lying on her bed reading it.

In adulthood, I continued to be drawn to a certain type of female advice-giver. I wanted women in black cashmere to tell me, in no uncertain terms, how to live my life. What recipes to make, what man to date, what haircut to try. This is one of the reasons that Nora Ephron is my favourite writer and eternal life guru – the advice in her journalism and personal essays is full of militant specifics (don't spend too much on a handbag, don't eat egg whites on their own, add more butter to the pan and more bath oil to your tub). I do not want smiley lifestyle vloggers with very white teeth and very sculpted faces to begin a video with 'Hey, guys' before telling me to try these sweet potato brownies 'that can be made non-vegan if that's what you like'. I don't want that at all. What I want is an imperious dame to tell me to get my shit together. I want a clever, funny, no-fucks-left-to-give woman to give me a list of seemingly random rules to make my life better. More efficient, easier and, above all, more pleasurable. I want her to tell me that I'm a fool if I don't follow these rules. This is something I find so difficult to receive from men, but give me a wise older woman in statement earrings telling me what she's learnt and I'll follow her to the ends of the Earth. If you can't find me at a wedding, and I'm nowhere to be seen by the cheeseboard or free bar, the chances are I am sitting at the feet of a grandmother or great-aunt, engulfed in Shalimar perfume and stories of lost love.

There is only one man whose life advice I've ever sought

out. During the *annus horribilis*, on one of my many sleepless nights, I wrote to Nick Cave. He writes a newsletter, The Red Hand Files, in which his fans write in to him and he answers in the capacity of a mystical and poetic agony uncle. Even during my years as an avid problem-page fan, I'd never actually written in to a stranger and asked for help. But there I was, some time in between midnight and dawn, typing away on my bed in the dark, asking Nick Cave to help me. I won't say what I asked, because it is too mortifying. And he never replied, but that didn't matter. What I learnt from sharing my most private pain with a semi-professional problem-solver was that the mere act of asking for help was, in itself, healing. It was as if I had crept down to the docks under the cover of darkness and floated a message out in a bottle, imagining how it might be received. By writing it I was acknowledging that someone might care about me; that they'd be able to say the right thing without knowing me. Because I was feeling something other people had felt and therefore I wasn't, as I'd suspected, the loneliest and strangest woman in the world.

Years ago I had quite literally begged for an advice column at another magazine (which I won't reveal except to say it was *Vogue*) but had been rebuffed. This was definitely for the best, as I recognize now that it's hard enough to receive advice from a thirty-something, let alone a twenty-something. But, aged 31, I managed to persuade my wonderful *Style* editor that this would be the right medium for me – a place where I could speak intimately to the reader, without necessarily speaking intimately about myself. Where I could give an opinion on people's emotions, rather than an opinion on the state of the world. In the first decade of my professional writing life, I'd written about all my fuck-ups, which I think is good training for an agony aunt. I couldn't and wouldn't claim to be a sage, or an expert, or even a person who made the right decisions. I would just be a person who'd made mistakes and was interested in learning. Someone who was trying to better understand life, just like the person writing in to me.

My first batch of letters was uncharacteristically zany. There was the woman who slept with a man 'almost immediately' after a first-date lunch, a retired male dentist whose kids were sick of him introducing them to his 'latest flames', a woman who was moving to Paris and was nervous about embarrassing herself in front of the locals as she liked to get 'biblically slaughtered' and a woman who feared she loved dogs more than men. A couple of years into doing this weekly column, I now know that the same problems come up over and over again every week (*they don't love me, I don't love them, I don't want to be friends with someone any more, my mum's annoying me*). It is why Claire Rayner, perhaps our most beloved advice columnist, apparently ended up categorizing problems and answers for efficiency (e.g. this letter is problem 45, needing answer 78). I like writing about these stalwarts of agony – there is something reassuring about their frequency and the fact we are all united in our own horribly unique pain. They're often the columns that get the most widespread sharing and responses. But you can't answer them over and over again without repeating yourself and then advice that was meant sincerely seems trite.

What I crave most are problems that are unusual – full of strange details that take you into the middle of a moral maze and really make you examine the best course of action. It's why one of my favourite letters was from a woman who had fallen in love with her mother's long-term boyfriend's son (effectively her step-brother). After having the best sex of her life with him, she was confused as to whether what they were doing was right or wrong or even legal (it was, the *Sunday Times* subeditors assured me). This was not a problem I had ever heard before, and I really had to think about where I stood. I lobbied the opinion of every colleague and friend in the week I was writing it, in order to interrogate all possible outcomes. These are the columns I get most excited about when I see them in my inbox. Although, I am haunted by an alleged story that an advice columnist for a national paper once earnestly answered a series of fantastically detailed and unusual problems, only to discover they were prank letters detailing the plots of famous films. E.g. 'I run an antiquarian bookshop in Notting Hill and I have fallen in love with a customer. The problem is, she has a very different job to me and lives in America. Should I pursue things?' Whenever I get a story that seems a little *too* zany, I always cross-check it with IMDb to make sure I'm not the punchline to an admittedly very funny joke.

Many of the problems I was sent in my first year of agony aunting were underpinned by Covid. I didn't want to keep referencing the pandemic as the reason for our misery as it felt obvious and a little, well, miserable. But I did think it was important to acknowledge its knock-on effect into unexpected areas of our exterior and interior lives, particularly as we were all so new to it. I received a lot of letters from people who had fallen out with family members because of differing politics, something that discussions of Covid made impossible to avoid. Agonizers wrote in describing their loneliness, sadness at missing out on life, fear they were not making the most of being young or single. Another recurring letter consisted of admissions from the long-married that they were thinking about their first love. This was both inevitable and relatable to me, someone who became an archivist of their own relationships during the lockdowns. Bereft of physical connection, I found comfort in the virtual. I read WhatsApp conversations with best friends that dated back to 2017. I scrolled back to the first photo on my iPhone in 2010 and flipped through my history like it was a glossy magazine in the hairdresser's. I googled the names of old boyfriends followed by 'LinkedIn' or 'JustGiving' to see if I could get back in touch with who they were and are, without getting back in touch with them.

As well as trying to avoid blaming Covid for everything, I also try to avoid going in too hard on the internet. I just can't read or watch much more about the evils of the internet. We all know that too much of it can be damaging. We all know that certain people can't use it healthily. The internet is like alcohol or driving or sex. We need to be taught its risks, how to use it safely, and I imagine our usage of it will one day be monitored and restricted. We're not there yet and, until we are, I don't think it's useful to begin too many sentences with: 'In the age of social media . . .' It's too lazy to outsource every problem to the presence of a digital world. I don't think our anxieties were invented by the internet. I just think the internet has given us a place to put them and make them multiply. And, in my past, lamenting on the downside of the internet, I have overlooked the ways it can enrich our lives. In my own life, I know lots of very happy couples who have met through dating apps or on social media. And, as my friends and I get older and find it increasingly difficult to find time for each other, I concede I would feel much less close to the people I love were it not for WhatsApp groups and 'close friend' stories on Instagram and shared albums of godchildren and shared calendars for us to work out how and when the hell we're going to meet up.

What I'm now interested in is how internet-related problems are the symptom of an underlying issue. That's what I always hope I can help a person diagnose. A recurring worry in the Dear Dolly inbox is one of missing out. I'm so often contacted by twenty-somethings who have just moved to London and worry that they're not having enough fun, or by single people who feel like they're not going on enough dates. Most commonly, I hear from women in relationships who are terrified that they aren't entirely fulfilled. Frightened that the choice they have made has closed off other, better possibilities, they want me to tell them whether the steadiness they've found with their partner is what a long-term relationship is meant to feel like, or whether it's actually just stagnancy and a lack of stimulation. There is an argument that this collective commitmentphobia has been aggravated by social media, the tyranny of constant comparison and our hyper-awareness of other potential opportunities. But I think the more compelling case is that commitment is simply harder when we live for so much longer; that the problem is exist-ential rather than digital. As our average life expectancy creeps slowly up to 90, meeting someone in middle age could still mean a fifty-year relationship. So of course the prospect of lifelong commitment is more daunting for us than it was for our grandparents, particularly when women have only very recently been able to explore the same sexual freedoms and career opportunities as men. This struggle between wanting a rooted, domestic existence and a life of nomadic liberty is a very human instinct, one that has been examined endlessly in the psyche of male stories and tormented male protagonists. Now, it's our turn to wres-tle with this quandary. It's one I'll never tire of exploring.

Exploration is always what I'm trying to do when I read and respond to letters. It is very rare that I give a clear-cut answer. When I interviewed Graham Norton and asked him about his time as an agony uncle, he told me that he always felt it was his job to imagine the viewpoint of the subject of the complaint. If someone writes in to talk about the distress caused by their friend, partner, family member or boss, it is easy to express sympathy and tell them that they're in the right. What is harder is to deliver a compassionate view from all sides. That, I feel, is the real toil of the agony aunt – to imagine what it is like for the people surrounding the agonizer. To extend your empathy to all parties. I try my best to do this in my replies – even when I disapprove of the person being written about, I try to imagine what might have made them behave that way.

There have been a few times when I have struggled to offer an alternate perspective to the agonizer, namely those who seem to be in relationships, friendships or family dynamics that are coercive or potentially danger-ous. In these instances, the safety of the person writing takes precedence over any attempts at an answer told with a 360-degree view. I once got a follow-up email from one of these letter-writers who told me that after she read my reply to her in the magazine, she ended her rela-tionship. It was a reminder of how seriously to take those letters when I do reply to them, which is rarely, because I am very aware that 'school of life' does not provide the necessary training to answer them.

The only topic I am steadfastly strident on is puritanism in all forms. I hate puritanism. And there's too much of it around these days. I don't like our phobia of excess and our fetish of restraint. I won't let someone be judgemental about their own eating or drinking or promiscuity, espe-cially if their judgement is clearly internalized from others. And, generally, I don't like people complaining about other people's lifestyles and personal habits. I'm also pretty intolerant of enforced career worship. Admittedly, I myself am pretty work-obsessed, but the older I get the more I realize that this is not the right choice for a lot of people. I don't think anyone should be judged for prioritizing their relationships and happiness over their job. And I don't like people complaining about their friends or partners not having as much ambition as them. Basically, I try to veer people away from attaching morality to things I don't deem as being achievements (e.g. being thin, rich, virginal or sober).

My unwillingness to moralize in each and every column is something a certain type of reader absolutely hates. The *Sunday Times* commenters, the regulars, turn up to the comment section every week and order the usual: a judgement. Who's right, who's wrong, who should get into trouble. They want a binary ruling on the person's ethics and, if I don't give it, they will fight it out amongst themselves below the column. Something I find quite fascinating is how high the engagement always is on any letter pertaining to fidelity. When a column goes live on the subject of cheating, the shares and comments are unusually multitudinous. Cheating or being cheated on is a sad but common experience – at some point in almost everyone's life it's likely we'll do it or it will be done to us. And yet, according to my readers, the unfairness of this fact of life still seems to be the thing that scandalizes us the most. In the absence of organized religion and its societal sanctions, we have newspaper comment sections instead.

I have long been plagued by a male commenter, whose name I won't mention because that's exactly what he wants, who chimes in every Sunday, sometimes just one minute after midnight when the online edition goes live, to announce that he is considering giving up his *Sunday Times* subscription on account of my column. His issue with my writing pre-dates the agony aunt column, so this threat of his has been looming for well over five years now. He just finds me so boring, that's his main gripe. He's endlessly bored by me. Occasionally, he writes his own version of how he'd advise the person writing in. I have now come to realize that he sees the comment section every Sunday as his own miniature column. I very much understand this inclination, and I'd probably be the same if I were him. So when I see other commenters congratulate him on the quality of his comment that week, I feel strange happiness for him and a mutual triumph for the pair of us.

Despite the occasional noisy detractor, I have always loved writing for the *Sunday Times*. As a feminist with liberal politics, it is a hugely privileged position to find yourself in as a writer. I have a direct line to Middle England. Every week when I sit down to write my column, I am excited by this prospect. I can sneak messages into the back page of the *Style* section, then that gets sneaked into houses in Hampshire. Judges and lawmakers and Tories may be reading my words over their toast and marmalade. I don't need to convince other left-leaning people my age that women shouldn't feel shame for having casual sex, or a person shouldn't hide the fact their ex-partner is trans. But I am always aware when I choose which letters to respond to that there's an opportunity to normalize subjects in households where they may still be stigmatized. And normalization is always more effective than instructing, not least because I still have so much to learn myself. I never, ever want to lecture people, but I do want to try to expand my empathy as an agony aunt (and human), and I hope readers want to join me too.

Most of the letters I get are from straight women writing in about men. I long for a more diverse range of issues from a more diverse range of letter-writers, but I can only respond to the people writing in (despite naysayers' insistence that the problems are made up by the editorial team – they're really not; if they were, they'd be much more varied, I promise). Occasionally, men write in to me, and I'm always struck by how differently their problems are structured. Women's letters mostly follow the template of: 'Here's my problem, here's why I think it's my fault, here's why I know it's not really a problem so I feel silly for writing to you, thank you for reading this, even writing it down has made me feel a bit better. Am I a bad person?' Whereas male agonizers tend to feel much more comfortable with placing blame on whoever they're writing about, and are confident in the fact that their problem really is a problem and one that is worthy of discussion.

Sometimes it's hard not to feel a bit blue about it all. If I were to look at the majority of letters I get week on week and put them all side by side, the story is one of female anxiety; of not feeling good enough. Of worrying that we're not being the right sort of girl from birth to death. Every decade of womanhood is marked by a new self-doubt.

It begins with teenage girls who hate the way they look, continues into early twenties with women who are anxious about having not lost their virginity yet, then they worry about why they've never had a relationship by their mid/ late-twenties and blame themselves. Then women get to their thirties and I'm inundated with messages of terror at the prospect that they'll never have children. Then they do have children and I get letters about being a terrible mother or a terrible friend because they can't balance a social life and family life. Then their children grow up and they worry about being terrible partners and wives. Then there are the letters of panic from women in their seventies writing in about their husband's erectile dysfunction and asking whether it's incumbent on them to spice things up.

When replying to all of these women, the first thing I always try to do is to take the shame out of their question. I think it's useful to remind the person that whatever it is they're experiencing, the likelihood is that other women have experienced it too. Which means they can focus on solving the problem rather than feeling self-loathing about it. I now understand that agony aunt trope of 'it's completely normal and perfectly healthy'. I never thought I'd be an it's-completely-normal-and-perfectly-healthy sort of woman. But here I am, your no-nonsense matron, telling you 'It's nothing I haven't seen before, girls.'

When appropriate, which is most of the time, I will then go on to explore how their personal problem is attached to societal sexism. If women write to admit they feel shame about their sex life or sexual past, or express hatred of their physical appearance, I think it's important to put it in its wider social context to fully understand where these feelings of self-doubt may originate. This is particularly relevant when I get my most common letter, which is from women who are terrified that they're not going to have children. I feel personally invested in this topic as the years I've spent writing the column have coincided with the period of my life where fertility scaremongering is inescapable. I want to do everything I can to provide women with the solace that I'm always looking for. To be reminded that a lot of fertility 'facts' are based on outdated and unsubstantiated science, that there is more than one way of having a family and that, most importantly, you never know how quickly your life is going to change.

These letters – the ones where women fear they aren't being the right kind of women – are the ones I find the easiest to respond to. My replies are an attempt at healing my own wounds as well as those of the women who've written to me. In putting together this collection, I went through every word of advice I've committed to print and I can see that, while I'm no longer a 'tell-all' writer, my most complicated emotions and my most sacred experiences hide in plain sight in these columns. Perhaps it is no coincidence that in the moment of my life when I thought I had a handle on nothing, I decided to advise strangers on everything. I could, in most cases, begin each response with: Dear Dolly. How very, very lucky I am that part of my job is being given the time and space to process life in this way.

Dating

1. Dating

2. Friendship

3. Relationships

4. Family

5. Sex

6. Break-ups
   & Exes

7. Body & Soul

Dear Dolly: 'Help! Men are put off by my height'

I keep on being rejected by men who, within a few months, start dating someone who is petite. I cannot help thinking that my height (5ft 11in) is what is putting these guys off. In the past I have been told that I am too tall to be considered 'sexy' and this has stuck with me to the point that I do not feel comfortable going on dates, especially with people I have been speaking to online. Help!

One of the strangest things about being a very tall woman is the frequent unpleasantness you face on account of your height versus the regularity of women telling you they're jealous of your height. 'Aren't you lucky?' petite pocket rockets the world over will say. Perfectly proportioned, average-sized, dinky little Disney-princess-faced ladies who have never had to shop in Long Tall Sally or known the sag of a gusset on a too-short pair of tights will tell you they would do anything to be your height.

The mythology about being a tall woman has, in the past, made me feel insane. If everyone wants to be this height, why do I not enjoy it? If being tall is so coveted, why am I so embarrassed about it all the time? Why do I feel so lumbering, inelegant, unfeminine and self-conscious? Why do I keep hearing that men love tall women, yet I have been told, time and time again, that someone wouldn't date me because I am taller than them?

There have been moments of vindication – nights out with friends where I wear a pair of high heels and they witness the relentless comments from strangers. The occasional 'lol, sorry 2 tall x' messages on dating apps. I will always remember watching an episode of *First Dates* that featured a man who said in his introductory clip, 'I. Hate. Tall. Girls,' only for a girl of my height to join him at the table with a big, hopeful grin on her face. 'When you walked in and you were taller than me,' he explained to her in the excruciating post-date debrief, 'it was an instant turn-off. It's nothing personal, but you may as well have been an ant. Like, a massive ant.'

So for that reason I am not going to lie to you. I'm not going to tell you that this is all in your head. You're right. There are men who won't be interested in you because of your height. And it sucks.

HOWEVER. Over the years I have found complete serenity in accepting this fact. Because here's who it *really* sucks for – it doesn't suck for us, the long-legged legends who can always see everything at a gig. It sucks for them. Because if a man has a problem with being with a woman who is taller than him, it's not that he thinks she's too big, it's because he thinks he's too small. He has been made to feel that he can't be a proper man, a good lover or benevolent protector for a woman without having substantial physical height over her. And that's a great shame. Those men shouldn't intimidate us or make us feel rejected, we should dig deep to find our compassion for them.

This all fell into place for me when, aged 23, I lay on the chest of the boy I was dating, my legs going on for miles after the point where his stopped, and in a drunken whisper he said: 'I'm sorry I'm not taller.' All his nasty digs about my height and his insistence that I always wore flat shoes around him suddenly made sense.

Here is another absolute truth, my solemn vow to you: just as there are men who wouldn't consider dating you because of your height, there are men who will find your height one of the sexiest things about you. Lots of them. They will revel in walking down the road with their arm around your shoulders or waist or arse or wherever they can reach. They will want you to wear heels all the time (*all the time*). They will think you are Wonder Woman (another 6ft-tall girl, incidentally). It will feel completely right and you will realize you should have felt nothing but pride about your height. An ex, months into dating, once showed me the text he sent his best friend from the loo during our first date:

'I am in love, she's ENORMOUS.' It made me so happy for my younger self. I wish I could have sent that text back in time to the self-loathing girl who genuinely googled 'shortening surgery'.

A final home truth from someone who has been there: there is absolutely nothing you can do to change this striking, unusual, beautiful thing about your body.

This is the only vehicle you have to take you right through to the end of your life. Please, please don't internalize those comments and make them facts – they're not. You will find someone who isn't intimidated by your height, someone who is turned on by stature and power, a man who is almost impossible to emasculate. And those guys, I promise, are always the most fun anyway.

Dear Dolly: 'I went on a double date with my housemate. I never stood a chance!'

I have just got back from a double date with my housemate, which was fun, but I felt she automatically put herself in the position of being the one to get with the fit boy we both fancied. She completely dominated the entire scenario (both of them matched with her online) and I never stood a chance to even consider which guy I wanted or who I vibed with most. What is the easiest way to say I don't like how you've treated me without coming across as whiny? My friend is very domineering and doesn't take it well when anyone disagrees with her.

OK, there are a lot of ingredients for a shit sandwich here, and I don't want to double-date victim-blame, but I think it might be helpful if we hold hands and together go through what went wrong. I have identified three key areas of danger.

1. Double dates as a concept

Let me tell you about the worst date of my life. The year is 2013. A male friend suggests we go out for dinner and that I bring a girl for him and he brings a boy for me. I take my housemate – a funny, beautiful, kind woman – knowing they'll get on famously. And they do, from the moment we arrive for drinks. I'm left hanging for an hour until a man in a tracksuit and beanie hat pulled down so low it's almost over his eyes finally lumbers in, drunk on whisky because 'Liverpool lost today'. He refuses to look me in the eye, let alone speak with me. We go to the restaurant, where my two friends continue to have a fantastic date. My guy turns his chair away from the table and spends the meal texting. He leaves before the bill is paid. The night ends back at my place – my housemate and my friend laughing and talking. She takes the guitar out, he sings 'Wicked Game' by Chris Isaak, she harmonizes. I watch on sullenly until I eventually go to bed alone.

It is hard enough for two people to have a successful date. It's even harder for two sets of couples to both have brilliant dates simultaneously. One person (minimum) is going to have a disappointing night. And yes, in principle, if your date is bad it's nice to have a friend there for moral support. But they're not going to be there for moral support if they're on a really good date. They're not going to be interested in you at all.

2. Going on a date with someone who once fancied/ still fancies your friend

A truly terrible idea. There are only a handful of things you need for a solidly good date: laughter, flirtation, mutual curiosity and letting one another know the other one's fit. This was not going to happen if the very reason these men came to be there is that they both matched with your friend on a dating app. Of course that's going to hang, said or unsaid, over the evening. You never had a chance, mate! There's nothing wrong with you – it's not that everyone fancies your friend and no one fancies you. This was doomed from the start.

And, yes, it was theoretically charitable of her to pass over this man to you like a dress she bought and decided she doesn't want to wear. And I'm sure there are people who do this with only good intentions. But it sounds like she's someone who would enjoy a situation where two men are fighting for her affection. If a woman ever magnanimously offers up an ex or a man she rejected as a romantic interest for you, think very carefully.

3. Going on a double date with a friend who is defined by being fancied

We've all known one of those women. And, in a way, it's not their fault. It's unsurprising that, having been culturally conditioned to seek male approval, some girls look for it at every turn. We understand it is a symptom of insecurity rather than arrogance; we show her compassion. But we also don't put ourselves in situations with her where we feel like we would be forced to compete for male attention (grim).

If this is part of a wider problem where you feel she

undermines you, then it's worth saying something. If you already know that she is a defensive person, don't lead with accusations (you do this, you are that), lead with vulnerable self-reflection that invites conversation (sometimes when I'm with you, I feel x-y-z and I'd like to talk about it because I am sure you would never want me to feel that).

But if this is just something that happened on a double date, my advice is never to go on a double date with her again. You have different friends for different things – maybe, for her own complicated reasons that are not your responsibility, she is not a good single-girl ally. Find another wingwoman.

In short: double dates are like a week clubbing in Ibiza or making a fondue at home. You do it once to say you've done it. Congratulations! Now you never have to do it again.

Dear Dolly: 'I'm addicted to unrequited love, and it's distracting me from actual dating. Will I ever have a healthy relationship?'

I think I'm a love addict. From the age of 11 (I'm now a 19-year-old woman), I have continuously and successively fallen in love with older women. They are women who I know I can never and will never be with, predominantly my teachers and lecturers. These infatuations are incredibly obsessive, not quite reaching into stalker territory, but not far off. Honestly, I feel insane, obsessively chasing the high of unrequited love with unattainable women, with my fantasies distracting me from actual dating. I'm scared that I'll never be able to have a healthy, committed relationship, and I'll forever remain a psycho.

I want to prefix this advice with a plain-as-day fact: some of the most important relationships of your teenage life will take place in your head. The stranger on the bus to whom you are married until they get off at their stop, the lecturer who is the protagonist of every masturbation fantasy, the random distant family member you see once every few years at a great-grandparent's birthday and then furiously google 'date with third cousin twice removed legal in UK?' – these are the romantic leads of your adolescence. And when you look back on these fantasy relationships in years to come, as strange as it sounds, they will almost hold the same weight in your memory as if they took place in real life. Obsession and imagination poured over the rocks of burgeoning sexuality is a powerful cocktail. You're not a psycho. I would be more surprised to hear from a 19-year-old who *doesn't* suspect they're a love addict.

That being said, your pattern of behaviour is an interesting one and worthy of analysis. By continually choosing to obsess over unattainable women, you are keeping yourself in a particular state of being single – one where you potentially cannot enjoy the freedoms of being young and unattached because you're preoccupied with the torture of unrequited love.

There are, of course, a number of simple explanations. You might be commitment-avoidant, which is understandable when you're 19. It could be that you're bored with your day-to-day life and so create vivid landscapes of fantasy. Perhaps you have incredibly high expectations for relationships, so you like to keep things fictional with someone unattainable so that your needs can be met in a one-sided way.

Digging a bit deeper, there is a possibility you're scared of a real and mutual connection with someone because you're scared of intimacy. What does that really mean? Here are a few expensive therapy sessions summed up in a sentence: intimacy means being seen and loved for all you are, while seeing and loving someone for all they are. If that sounds full-on, it's because it is. You have to know yourself before you can allow someone else to know you too. Maybe you're still working that out. I'd prioritize that above everything else at this stage.

Because these romantic fixations can be a monopoly on your time and mind — which is fine if you're fine with that — what you've got to watch out for is if it starts taking something from your self-worth. You don't have to be a particular 'kind of girl' to be loved: you aren't lacking in qualifications, you aren't better suited to unrequited crushes. Indulge in these fantasies if they give you a thrill, but try to keep them in perspective. Don't let insecurity and exhaustion become the default place for you to dwell.

I think the most likely reason as to why you're forming attachments to these unreachable women is that you're trying to avoid reality. And why wouldn't you? You have just entered adulthood and you're probably beginning to realize that reality is disappointing. You are entirely correct! As long as you're aware that these obsessions aren't indicative of what a loving, respectful, sustainable relationship is, I see no harm in your fantasies. (Although don't turn up on anyone's doorstep. Fill your notebooks with thoughts of them, stuff your web history with searches of their name, plus 'age', 'married', 'naked', 'net worth'. But that's your lot.)

The fact that you are worrying about this and thinking of how it might affect your chance of a committed relationship means you have an immense self-awareness that many of us lack. It is clear from your letter that you're accepting accountability for your actions and emotions, which means you're already taking good care of your future self. There is always a gap of time between recognizing a bad habit and changing it. So, for now, run riot in that gap if it feels fun. Enjoy the intensity, drama and madness of these obsessions while you still have the energy. Trust me, one day you'll realize you've tired yourself out.

Dear Dolly: 'How can I stop being a foster girlfriend?'

I am a 'foster girlfriend'. I am the girl before the boy finds a serious girlfriend and his forever home. How can I stop being the one in the situationship but not the relationship? Most recently, the guy I've been dating for the past six months has just hit me with the 'I don't want a relationship, but I love hanging out with you' chat, yet he's the one who has been acting like a boyfriend! I'm so fed up with being 'that girl'. I'm sure it makes me look cool and laid-back to his friends, but it's actually very boring, and I feel like I am just waiting around for them to decide, and when they do decide, it's not me.

Confused in Clapham

(Please keep me anonymous, as I know he has a Times *subscription)*

First and foremost, let me reassure you that this is a common dating pattern for so many women I know who are between the ages of 25 and 35. They incubate a man in a state of evident-yet-unsaid partnership, before being told by him several months in that he is not ready to commit. Then, a year later, up comes the Instagram post of the very same man on a Dubai beach with a woman next to him brandishing her hand at the camera and the caption: 'Marriage with this one has a nice *ring* to it!!!!'

My overarching dating theory is that most men crave being single, but are terrible at actually being single. I support this sweeping statement with Oedipal ideology that the wordcount of this column will not withstand, so, in short: a lot of men think they're being single, when they're actually just jumping from one pretend mini-relationship to another. It's like they're doing frenzied emotional parkour, confusing every landing place as they go on their pathetic little adventure. Then suddenly, one day, they get tired and just stop on the roof they last found themselves on. This is the worst behaviour in dating. The serial daters who are very clear they will be offering no more than one text a week and a possible strain of herpes are – in my opinion – chivalrous in their own way.

Here's the annoying fact about love, which is unromantic, unsatisfying and unfair, but it might help you rationalize why this keeps happening: compatibility is only a small factor for whether two people will go on to have a relationship. It's ridiculous, I know. It should be as simple as: we're both available and we really like each other, so let's give this a go. But it's not. It's far more complicated than that. Not only do you have to meet someone who you really like and who really likes you too, but also you must have both arrived at a specific moment of availability. This readiness is decided by our own minds, but we let ourselves believe it is dictated by our personal past, future and the laws of timing.

On any given day thousands of perfectly lovely relationships are not happening because one party has decided it's not the right time for them. When a person's yellow taxi light is off, there's absolutely nothing you can do to convince them to switch it on. And neither should you – it's humiliating for you and an unfair demand on them. No one is obliged to be in a relationship when they don't want to be in one.

I think you keep meeting people who haven't got their yellow light on, but they behave in a way that makes you think they have, because they want a trip with you. The only thing you can do is be upfront fairly early on about the fact you are looking for a relationship. Don't worry that this is too much to load on someone – it's not. It is a responsible way to date. And hopefully it means you will be able to detect who is unavailable in the beginning stages, so you don't waste your time and heartache on them.

And here's another explanation you might want to explore: are you dating men who are in the first ten months out of a big relationship? Because that makes you a number-one target to be a foster girlfriend. If you meet someone who has recently gone through a break-up, I would think carefully before you invest a substantial amount of time in them. It's hard, because people who are fresh out of painful relationships are often the most irresistible, because they're in such a fun and newly carefree state: the most likely to order shots on the first date, go to pop-up bars in car parks and loot Lovehoney of all its battery-operated two-person devices. What makes it even harder is they often seem like they're committing to you because they're not used to being single, so they carry the intimacy forward from their last partner.

Most people, however, think of their first encounter after a break-up as a holiday, where they can be a 'yes' person with no responsibilities. It doesn't matter how well you get on, they'll regard your relationship as a finite experience. You, I'm sorry to say, will always be Lanzarote to them. Go back through the last men you've dated and check whether they were recently single. That could be your answer – you might have unwittingly been the sandy beach where they can recline in between the destination of their last relationship and the destination of their future one.

And, last, you might find it helpful to know that, in all my years of field research, I have continuously found Clapham to be the place where the worst men in London congregate. It might be an idea to move. Or if you're fond of the Common and the high density of Gail's Bakeries, then stay put for the greenery and pain aux raisins, but go elsewhere to look for love.

Dear Dolly: 'I fall in love with every man I meet. How do I stop?'

I fall in love with everyone. If a male co-worker is nice to me, I then feel genuine heartbreak when he goes on a date. I go to a party and feel like the night is a failure if no one hits on me. I serve a flirty customer and all I can think about is if they'll ask for my number and then I feel pain in my chest if they don't. I imagine scenarios in my head with people after one conversation. Every song or movie reminds me of an ex or someone I went on one date with. How can I stop feeling love × 1,000 about every male?

Do you want the good news or the bad news first? I'm a glass-half-overspilling gal myself, so I always opt for the good news. OK, I'll give you the good news.

The good news is, you have an imagination bursting out of your brain like a single bridesmaid in a dress a size too small. What a gift that is! I know at the moment your compulsive delusions feel embarrassing, but I don't think you know just what a superpower it can be. You can physically stay in this earthly realm while your mind checks out and leaves for an entirely different place. You can be in the Caribbean while you stand in a queue for the post office. You can be in love while you brush hands with a particularly hot cashier. You can create whole parallel universes with just the power of your grey matter – writing conversations and embroidering details of personality and building relationships between strangers. You are an architect of fantasy! You are a master of imagined worlds!

What are you going to do with all these stories? You can paint them or perform them. Jot them down as a collection of private thoughts or put them in a song. You can, quite literally, type them into a Word document or a Final Draft file and reimagine all the encounters of your life had they gone a different way. I highly recommend it. You could have a lot of fun.

And now for the bad news. As joyful as fantasy can be – as essential as I believe it is for the sanity of many – it should never become more important than reality. The scenes in your head shouldn't be more meaningful than the scenes of your life. You should never place all your self-worth and happiness in the hands of someone you barely know. The direction of your day should not spike or plummet depending on whether a stranger shows you a bit of attention. If it does, then it means there is a problem.

It might be that you're just a bit bored. Maybe you need to shake up your life a bit. This doesn't have to be anything drastic, but it seems like you might need to find some other ways of being stimulated. Personally, I have found that nothing cuts short a protracted daydream about Timothée Chalamet like an extremely jam-packed schedule. Could you throw yourself into a creative project? Take a course? Learn a new skill? Join a dating app? Actively try to meet some new people? Save up and plan for a trip?

And if you're not bored, maybe you're suffering from low self-worth. If you artificially fall in love with numerous people every week, you also make yourself vulnerable to artificial heartbreak. I use the word artificial carefully, because I know that the power of your mind means these interactions feel super-intense, and that is very real. But I worry that you are as addicted to the imagined rejection as you are the imagined longing. If that's true, why? Is it possible that, just as you form made-up stories about men, you've also created one about yourself? Have you decided that you are someone who won't ever find love? Are you trying to look for anecdotal evidence to fortify this theory so you can continue knowing you are undeserving of love?

You are probably always going to be someone who gets lost in their romantic mirages. That's OK. It's lovely to be a dreamer. But you have to find a way of not torturing yourself with these flights of fancy, or using them as proof that you don't deserve to be with someone who loves you back. Every time you become obsessed with these fantasy boys, you are falling in love with your own imagination. That's not about connection and love. That's not about anyone other than you.

You obviously have a lot of love to give and one day you'll find someone who really deserves to receive it.

He'll be real and here and you can love the hell out of him. You'll know the map of his freckles. You'll always have his favourite cereal in your cupboard. Every Lionel Richie lyric will finally make sense. All that frantic, horny, obsessive, beautiful, gentle love will have somewhere to go. So don't spend too much time in your head. You might miss him.

Dear Dolly: 'I'm worried I love dogs more than men'

I'm worried I am unable to form successful, deep relationships with men. I was married for fifteen years to a gentle, sweet man who I met when I was young and naive. I thought I was in love with him, and we had many happy years bringing up our children, surrounded by our dogs. But there was a void in our relationship and a loneliness inside me: I always felt like our dogs understood me better than he did.

Since then I have had two relationships. The first was with a man who seemed to be wonderful. He had a lovely elderly dog who got on well with my two dogs. For two years all was good. Then his dog died. Almost instantly he annoyed me. Without his dog, the attraction wasn't there. He wasn't keen on coming on dog walks any more, and we seemed no longer to have anything in common.

The second relationship lasted for eighteen months. I fell for him in a big way and I truly thought we were good together. He has two dogs. I was very much looking forward to seeing him again after a long time apart in lockdown, but I have to admit that when I arrived at his house the lump in my throat occurred not on seeing him, but when his dogs came bounding over to me. Their love is so honest and straightforward compared with all his complications.

Can a man ever give me the feeling of unconditional love and understanding that I feel with dogs? Have I always fallen in love with men's dogs and not actually with them? Should I make sure the next relationship I have is with a man who does not have a dog?

A lot to unpack here.

I don't think you should be worried that you can't form relationships with men. You've described three relationships, one that lasted for fifteen years in which you raised children together. Your concern is that you can't form deep relationships with men – a depth you are able to reach easily when it comes to dogs. But I think what you're searching for is simplicity, rather than depth.

Look, I love dogs. If there's a dog at a party, I find it. I've fallen to my knees in Regent's Park on sight of a particularly bouncy golden retriever like I was meeting the Pope. I spend a lot of time on the Battersea Dogs & Cats Home website. I get it. But I have always been slightly wary of those who say that they prefer the company of a dog to a person. The love a dog gives you is unconditional, as you say, but it is nothing like the sort of unconditional love that can occur between humans. Our pets are devoted to us because we care for them; because we are more familiar to them than any other figure in their world. And we love our pets because it is an uncomplicated set-up; ritualized with physical gestures rather than conversation. Crucially, they don't talk back to us.

I wonder if that is what you're craving when you look for romance. Someone who responds to orders, who gives you affection all day and night, who doesn't make you look inwards or hold you accountable for your actions. I see the appeal, but it's going to be a hard dynamic to find outside of S&M role play. I'm guessing from some quick maths that you're middle-aged and, unless you're looking for a toy boy, finding silent and steadfast subservience in a straight man aged over 50 is going to be even harder.

There is a possibility you don't want a partner at all. I know plenty of women who were in a long relationship while they raised a family, separated when the children were grown up, and the minute they were on their own all romantic inclination left them. It's as if, after years and years of searching for love, finding love, retaining that love, then a whole new love bursting out of them when they had children, they were just loved out. If that's the case for you, you shouldn't worry. You should enjoy a new phase of your life where you have no one to care for when you open the door to your home, other than you and your dogs.

If you do want a relationship, be honest with yourself about what personality traits are important to you. It seems like you tend to misjudge your compatibility with men because you get distracted by what will hereon in be referred to as The Dog Stuff. It is easy to overstate the significance of a person being an animal lover as evidence of moral purity. Just because someone cares about animals does not mean they extend that empathy to their fellow man. Look at Morrissey. He would be absolutely delightful to your dogs. But I don't want you to date him.

When you meet someone, irrespective of whether they're a dog owner, make sure you spend the majority of time getting to know each other at the start, away from all The Dog Stuff. It will help you to gain clarity on who they really are. Beyond this specific example, I think we all can get too caught up in shared interests as a defining factor for whether a relationship will work. Passions and hobbies can give you a shared language and schedule, but I'm not sure if those things form a rock-solid foundation for love. Your partner needs to make you laugh and turn you on. You need to find their thoughts and conversation interesting. You should get a kick out of their company when it's just the two of you.

I'd be interested to know what your dogs' take on all this is, though.

Dear Dolly: 'I'm a feminist – so why am I only attracted to misogynists?'

I am a 29-year-old woman and, having spent the majority of my twenties in a long-term relationship, I have now spent the past three years exploring my sexuality. This has mainly consisted of sleeping with 'cool' and 'hot' men who are unattainable and completely emotionally unavailable. In a recent counselling session the penny finally dropped that I am, in fact, almost solely sexually attracted to misogynists. Ironically, I am a staunch feminist – misogynists represent everything I hate about the patriarchy. How do I stop being drawn to them and start feeling sexy with 'nice' men instead?

Hello! Thank you for coming! Nice to have you here. Please help yourself to your free welcome drink and join us in Function Room 3 in five minutes along with the other confused feminists for the first seminar of the day: 'How will I feel when they stop wolf-whistling *really*?'

Take it easy on yourself. This is an internal battle fought by many self-respecting women. God knows why. For some, it is a self-esteem issue – a subconscious belief that they are not worthy of kindness. Others might have become so used to objectification that it's the only thing they recognize as romantic attention. Some confuse that attention with love. Maybe the rest of us are just into horrible men because we were signed up to the Patriarchy Cult from birth without our knowledge. And even once we try to leave, its values are so destructive it takes a while to deprogramme ourselves.

But you can find a safe place to put these desires. You can keep it in a fantasy realm. You can want to be respected by a partner and you can also wish to not be respected when you're in bed together. You can ask for both of those things and it doesn't make you a hypocrite. It doesn't make you a bad feminist. It doesn't make you a messed-up person. It just means you're a woman with a sexual appetite – some of which you understand and some of which you don't.

Personally, I think our sexual identity is something we should all be allowed to enjoy and explore (safely, legally and consensually) guilt-free and without neuroses. I don't think intricate analysis of preference and practice is required for most of us. I don't think you need to complicate a sexual inclination with a quest to find its origins unless it interests you. And if you enjoy objectification or even degradation in bed, you should find a safe way to do that. And you should not give yourself a hard time about it.

You had the same sexual partner for most of the first phase of young adulthood – it's perfectly understandable that you're now trying out stuff. It might be that you're attracted to dangerous or unknowable men as a reaction to having been in a loving relationship. Perhaps it feels like a novelty after being in something so steady and secure. I also wonder whether you're enjoying being single, therefore you keep choosing to date men who you know won't be a viable choice for a long-term relationship or who won't commit to you at all.

If that is the case, allow yourself the possibility of being single for the foreseeable future and let yourself enjoy that. Don't feel shame about it and don't let it panic you about the possibility of love in the future. You have been in a stable relationship with a suitable man, you will be able to do it again. If you're not ready for it yet, you can date casually or be promiscuous and do it in a way that doesn't harm you or others. Join a dating app, be clear about what you're looking for and find other people who also just want a fling, but who are nice to you as well. Please, please believe me when I tell you: it's not just the nasty men who will know how to turn you on.

It's great you're being so thoughtful about how your choices reflect your beliefs, but I also think you don't have to moralize your sexuality. What we find hot in fantasy is often an inversion of what we want in reality — transgression and taboo are a part of that. Honestly, I think everyone should be free to separate their sexuality from their politics, as long as every party has consented and is having fun.

What's important is that you don't confuse your craving for sexual objectification or domination with a need for a misogynistic or dominating boyfriend. I know you already know this, but just in case you need reminding: you deserve to be listened to, admired, championed, cared for, taken seriously and cherished. You don't have to sacrifice sexual voracity for those things. Put simply: you need a kind, chill, respectful boyfriend in the streets and a filthy pervert in the sheets. They do exist. I hope you have fun finding one.

Dear Dolly: 'Do I give up on dating charismatic men and instead settle for Mr Nice?'

Last year an intense, short-lived relationship came to an end, as he went from saying that I meant the world to him to then abruptly ending things because he might travel this year. (Ha to him for that one.) But he was a rare find of a man (especially at 24), as he thought deeply about things, had a crystal collection (that he was proud of), was ambitious at work, all while still having a good time partying at weekends. I really cared about him. So when I spotted him in town, I decided to message him to check in. Not only did he not reply, but also he removed me from his social media. It stung and sent me into a spiral of trying to answer the agonizing question: 'Do I give up on dating charismatic men and instead settle for Mr Nice?'

Lots of love,

Quarter Life Crisis

If there is one good thing that has come out of this global pandemic, it is that at least everyone knows their ex is having a horrible time. I think it might be the greatest unspoken silver lining and one I'd like to celebrate

31

for a moment. While before it was always faintly possible that your ex-boyfriend was in a hotel suite somewhere having a threesome with Miss Sweden and Miss Brazil, at least now you know for certain that he's in his flat watching *Chernobyl*, miserably eating yet another bowl of penne and Dolmio. I am very pleased that your ex didn't get to go travelling this year, Quarter Life Crisis, and even more pleased that he was stuck indoors with nothing but his crystal collection for company.

Now, these crystals. I think they should be our jumping-off point. I wonder why it is that when you describe this man so adoringly, the crystal collection and his pride in it is something you immediately recall. The list of traits you assign to him feels almost like you're describing a character in a script: 'DAN, 24, deep thinker, ambitious but likes to party, stares thoughtfully into his amethyst as he sips a double espresso.' I think you might be a romantic, which is a great thing, but it could also mean you overestimate or overanalyse a person's characteristics in order to cast them in the self-penned future scenes of your life.

The fact that this man owns crystals and works hard at his job doesn't really tell you anything about who he is or how he was going to treat you. I wonder if you missed any warning signs because you were distracted by his various interests that you assumed made him more compatible with you than he was. This is not at all an excuse for his garbage behaviour, and I do not want to load any of the blame on to you, but I think if you are able to examine your prospective partners a little more keenly in the future, you might be more likely to protect yourself from heartbreak. A tendency to over-romanticize relationships means you are full of optimism and hope, which is not something you want to lose. But it is something you are going to have to be aware of and manage if you want to be alert to when someone might potentially hurt you.

It is easier said than done, particularly in an age when nearly everyone's personalities are registered and displayed on social media profiles like they're a business at Companies House. But when you meet someone, it's so important to home in on the reality of them rather than the ornamentation of them. How do they communicate with you? How do they speak about others? Do their actions align with their sentiments, or is their affection for you restricted to big declarations and nothing else?

But there is also no guarantee that hyper-awareness will have a 100 per cent success rate. People who are largely good are still capable of being cruel or selfish when it comes to romance. People who give monthly donations to charity may well cheat on their partner. Just because a man likes the soulful and searching lyrics of late-1960s Dylan does not mean that he's going to worship you like the woman in 'Lay Lady Lay'. Soft bois who collect crystals might also dump you, ignore your texts and remove you from their social media.

My point is, you can so rarely summarize all of a

person by these surface signifiers of their tastes and habits. The best way to approach dating, particularly in your early mid-twenties, is with an open mind – be curious to find out who someone is and willing to be surprised by who might be a good match for you. While self-knowledge is the thing we're told is the key to contentment, I also think it is something we shouldn't be seeking as a conclusion. Finding a one-line story to summarize yourself or others can halt your own development, so try to avoid absolutes about who you are or who your perfect partner is. I know that story-boarding your life feels like you have entire control over its future plot, but as hard as you may try, you don't.

And you don't need to settle for anyone. Enjoy the process of meeting lots of people and having all kinds of encounters and relationships. Try not to caricature men into a binary of either being kind and boring or charismatic and dangerous. My friend Lauren has been in a relationship for more than a decade and she wrote the best line I've ever read on long-term love: 'It's not the absence of fun, it's the absence of fear.' Keep this in mind when you are looking for someone to share your life with – someone who'll bring fun without fear. Someone whose company you love. Someone who makes you feel alive and safe and understood. Those are the specifics you should be looking for. The rest doesn't matter so much.

Friendship

1. Dating

2. Friendship

3. Relationships

4. Family

5. Sex

6. Break-ups
   & Exes

7. Body & Soul

Dear Dolly: 'I need help breaking up with a friend'

I need help breaking up with a friend. 'Emma' and I have been friends since we were children and we're now in our mid-twenties and have been living together for about a year. We've got a little longer left on our contract, but when that's over I think I want to both physically and mentally distance myself from her. We've had no serious bust-up, it's been a slow and uncomfortable series of arguments, snide remarks and passive-aggressive WhatsApp messages that have led us here. Though she has always supported me through break-ups, work issues and money trouble, I feel like my life would be calmer and simpler without this friendship. Do I owe her an explanation, though I can't fathom exactly what's gone wrong between us myself? Would it be wrong to simply ghost her?

I have been in the handing-out-unwarranted-advice game since I acquired language, and the agony-aunting game for just over four months now. Every week my editor sends me a selection of letters from which to choose, and I file them all into a document. There are the very specific questions ('Should I send my ex something I made in my pottery class?'), there are some that do not require a page's worth of rumination ('Should I get a fringe cut?') and then there are the same problems that appear in different guises every single week. Without fail there is always a woman worrying about how to break up with a close friend.

I say this to reassure you – it is one of the most common relationship anxieties, and yet is so mired in guilt. I think we worry that a finished friendship always means failure, when actually it can mean freedom. If a friendship can't evolve as its two participants mature and change, it's likely that they'll grow out of it. This doesn't mean that it hasn't enriched you and it doesn't make your memories null and void. Your relationship and shared story is an achievement (childhood to mid-twenties – that's longer than the median length of a marriage!). It just may not serve you any longer.

But before you work out an exit strategy, I think you need to do some forensics on the friendship. You say that you don't know why you've drifted apart, but the timeline suggests that the problems began when you moved in together. The issues you mention – arguments, passive-aggressive WhatsApp messages – reek of domestic quarrelling. (I lived with housemates for seven years and I am more than familiar with the 'Hey just went to get my Marmite out of the cupboard and noticed a recent knife mark in it that I don't recognize??? Would be great if someone could clear this up????' texts.) It could be that you're describing an incompatible flatmate rather than an incompatible friend. If so, you may find that not living together returns your relationship to a relaxed and respect-ful place without confrontation. Some friendships simply can't withstand flat-shares – there are many people in my life who I adore, but there aren't enough jars of Marmite in Christendom to get me to live with them.

If you absolutely know that the friendship has natur-ally come to an end, I would still avoid a big goodbye speech. Those conversations, which are basically one person telling the other one all the things that are wrong with them, can be traumatic. Anyone who has had a friend explain exactly why they don't want to be friends any more can attest that the reasons never quite leave you (thanks, ********* ***** in Year 9 during that lunch break). The fact that you don't know exactly why you've become distant means it's probably more mutual than you think – those dynamics of long-term relationships rarely change without both parties being aware of it.

Which doesn't mean you should ghost her. That is both cruel and cowardly. What I suggest instead is a slow and subtle cooling-off period, which often happens after two people move out of a shared home anyway. If she is hurt or asks for answers, then you should be honest with her. Do this kindly – describe the changes you've noticed in your friendship, rather than the flaws you see in her. Tell her that you cherish everything she has given you, but that you think the friendship might have run its course. If she doesn't agree, there's an opportunity for a conversation in which you both share your feelings and find a way to communicate clearly again.

And while I don't think you should retain a friendship with someone who makes you unhappy, I do encourage you to be open to adaptation rather than a break-up. Friendships can change to become healthy without ending entirely. It might be that you share less with each other, she might become someone you see twice a year on your respective birthdays. History alone can't hold a friendship together, but it does become something you value more and more as you get older. One day, to your surprise, you may find she's the only person you want to call. And you might not be best friends, but you'll be happy to hear each other's voice.

Dear Dolly: 'My friends all earn more than me and I can't keep up'

I have a group of close friends I've known since school. As we've grown up, they have all begun to earn significantly more than me. It means they have been lucky enough to be able to buy their own homes, have lovely meals out and take expensive trips, whereas I find myself constantly budgeting and struggling to keep up with their lifestyles. I don't want to stop being friends with them, but I'm embarrassed that I can't always afford to do what they do, and I feel like I'm being left behind. What should I do?

Years ago one of my best friends agreed to meet up with a male friend of hers for a pint in Soho. My friend, at the time in her mid-twenties, was not skint but her salary was modest and every evening had to be budgeted to accommodate the cost of her London rent and travel. Her friend, who worked in theatre, got a text from an actor asking if they'd like to join a group of them in a Pizza Express. My friend knew she couldn't really afford dinner out but agreed as she didn't want to cut the night short. When she arrived she was greeted by a heaving table of actors and directors, one of whom was the *Twilight* star Robert Pattinson. She immediately knew she was out of her financial depth, so ordered a prudent plate of dough balls and a glass of tap water. When the bill came they split it. My friend knew she didn't have enough money in her account to pay her portion, but didn't want to seem like a party pooper by suggesting everyone pay for what they ordered. She went to the loo, had a meltdown and decided it would be best to pretend she'd lost her debit card. And it was there, under the blue glow of the Pizza Express lights as she watched Robert Pattinson kindly pay for her dinner of eight balls of plain dough, that she wondered how she'd ever got herself into such a tangle.

It is a sign of your good nature that you are trying to avoid uncomfortable conversations in your friendship group, but 'keeping up' with people's lifestyles is never, ever something you should feel pressured into doing. You shouldn't feel any embarrassment about not earning what your friends earn. It's obvious to say, but salaries and subsequent lifestyle are not always indicative of talent or hard work. The allocation of high-earning jobs is often down to lots of other factors too: privilege, timing, sheer dumb luck. We should always be aware of that fact, no matter what we earn, and be sensitive to various incomes within a friendship group so that no one feels ashamed or excluded.

I am sure your friends are lovely people, and I'm sure they would be mortified to know how oblivious they've been to your worry. I think the likelihood is that, because they are all in a similar earning bracket, they assume you are too. Or, having earned well for a while, they've forgotten what it's like to calculate the cost of a dough ball.

Money is an icky topic, even with the people who are closest to you, but it has to be talked about. Something I have learnt as I've got older is that the best way to avoid confusion or upset about money is to have one very frank conversation in order to not talk about it again. It is what's unsaid that causes distress. If you're lending or borrowing money within a family or friendship group, there needs to be an (inevitably awkward) honest discussion of how it's going to work, so it can then be forgotten. Before a group holiday, everyone needs to be clear about what they can and can't afford, so the holiday can be enjoyed. I think you need to have one of these conversations with your friends.

I know it feels humiliating, and you really shouldn't have to explain your finances to anyone other than your accountant, but it will lift a huge pressure off you. All you need to say is that you love spending time with them but you've become aware that they have more disposable income than you do, and you'll need to do some cheaper activities with them if you all want to hang out.

They might offer to pay for you to include you in more expensive experiences – whether you feel comfortable accepting that is entirely up to you. If you don't, be prepared that they might continue to do those things without you. I think that's fine if it's occasional, as they're allowed to enjoy their salaries and shouldn't feel guilty about that. But they should make an effort also to have more inclusive experiences.

What's important is that they realize that the people are what make an evening or holiday memorable, not the price of it. Some of my happiest memories with my friends have cost the price of a Domino's pizza on the sofa or a tinnie on a beach. It's fun to experience luxury with loved ones, but it's also not important. If they're good people they will know that too.

Dear Dolly: 'My best friend didn't pick me to be a bridesmaid'

My best friend didn't pick me as one of her six bridesmaids — how do I not feel upset? I am finding the realization that she means more to me than I do to her very hard. I know that the choice of bridesmaids can sometimes be a political and diplomatic decision, but I am finding it tough not to take it personally.

I have a friend, let's call her Jill, who was organizing a wedding. When it came to choosing her bridesmaids, she felt she had to ask the girl she had been drifting apart from for years (let's call her Anne). She felt like not asking Anne would mean a huge confrontation, which she didn't want, as it was obvious that their friendship was unsalvageable. The easiest option was just to make her a bridesmaid. 'I think my wedding might be the last time I ever see Anne,' she declared defeatedly. She made sure Anne stood at the end of the wedding party line-up in every photo, so she could be cropped out at a later date. The other bridesmaids privately renamed Jill's wedding 'Anne's leaving do'.

I tell this story not because I think your relationship with your friend is similar to Anne and Jill's, but because it demonstrates how much we look to the role allocation at weddings as a couple's public appraisal of their friendships. We've all nervously waited for the call-up to tier one (maid of honour, godparent). We've all known the sharpness of being relegated to tier two ('You're very special to us, so we'd like you to be: MC/reader of a psalm/ring bearer'). Some of us unmarried and childless folk (ahem) have, at times, resented this friendship census that couples are allowed to conduct, and wondered how they would feel if we officially employed our friends to do jobs of varying importance for an upcoming birthday party in accordance with how much we love them.

I'd love to tell you this means nothing but of course it means something, and I can see why you're feeling wounded. But, as you recognize yourself, weddings are often political, complicated and messy.

If there's one thing I've learnt about weddings, it's that if there is a big party then it is not being funded by the couple. And if it's not being funded by the couple, the couple aren't getting a say in most of it. This means very random people can become very important in the day's proceedings. For example, if the groom has a sister, I'm always staggered by her prevalence at a wedding and its surrounding anticipatory events. Her role is so nebulous, and yet she often becomes an instant bridesmaid. Not to generalize, but I've found she is nearly always a very rude person who runs her own crocheted brooch business. She has little to no relationship with the bride, and yet the bride will spend most of the hen do and wedding with her glued to her side.

There is also the possibility that your friend feels that if she asked you to be a bridesmaid, it would mean she would have to ask another person or people who she would deem to be the same level of friend as you, or who is associated with your friendship group. I've heard a lot of brides talk about this being a very real problem, because they don't want their bridesmaid count to reach double figures. They worry that the role of bridesmaid is rendered meaningless if the group amounts to the same headcount as a hockey team.

Another possibility (this one is a bit ouchie) is that she might have decided you wouldn't fit the role of bridesmaid for a reason she has invented. I know a girl who was told by her oldest friend that she wouldn't be a bridesmaid because she didn't want her to 'pull focus' on the day (the girl in question is exceedingly charismatic, drinks a lot and is very photogenic). I'm not saying this is fair or right, but I think it's worth remembering how much pressure women can put on themselves to have a perfect wedding day and be the perfect bride, and how much this can warp their judgement.

And, yes, if you had always thought she would be one of your bridesmaids, there is also a possibility that she is a closer friend to you than you are to her. To which I ask: is she good to you? Does she understand you and support you? Do you have a laugh together? If the answer to all the above is yes, then so what if you rank each other with different official terms? That's OK! She just might have a larger or longer-spanning group of friends.

That doesn't mean she doesn't love you enormously. And it shouldn't change how you hold her in your heart.

Plus, a silver lining: no jobs on the day! No carrying crates of tealights to the venue at the crack of dawn! No flower crown! Wear a ridiculous outfit, drain that parent-funded free bar and make sure you have a dance with the bride, because it sounds like you love her.

Dear Dolly: 'How do I support my single friends when I'm in a relationship?'

Half of my friends are single and the other half have settled down. I'm somewhere in the middle, happily in a three-year relationship in my mid-twenties. My question for you is about how to support my single female friends. One recently told us she didn't want to tell our friendship group (of five, four in relationships) about her most recent break-up as she felt like a failure compared to us. This broke my heart — I was single for a long time before my current boyfriend and completely remember the feeling. What do I say or do to help?

I have never really had a huge number of single friends. Nearly all my best friends have been in relationships since their mid-twenties, whereas I've spent most of my life single. Over the years we've all had to learn (and continue to learn) how best to support each other as our lives play out on wildly differing trajectories. I feel very lucky to be surrounded by coupled-up women who are, for want of a better term, single allies; who value my life as highly as theirs even though it is one without the things they all have in common. That you're aware that being single has its challenges and you want to know how to support your friends through them means you're already a very lovely friend. Any single woman would be lucky to have you in her life.

I think one of the things that's most overlooked in friendships between single and non-single friends is how important it is to populate each other's worlds equally. Because milestones are still culturally valued so highly (marriage, mortgages, children) it means that those going through them often become the focus of the friendship group.

Of course it is an honour for single people to celebrate those rites of passage of the women they love and, in turn, become enmeshed in their domestic lives. But it can feel isolating when that same enthusiasm and interest is not reciprocated. Try to stay aware of keeping that balance in your friendship group because (trust me) if you don't the default will fall in favour of those in relationships.

Every time your single friend has dinner with you and your boyfriend, make sure you have dinner with her and someone who is important in her life – maybe that's her best friend from work or her sibling. Every time she goes to the home you share with your partner, make sure you go to her flat where she lives with housemates or alone. If one day you have children and she comes round to play with them, you should, in turn, think of a way in which you can show her the same level of care.

It's also just a simple act of acknowledging your privilege. You're not more privileged than her because you have a partner, but you do have a different experience of the world, which is still mostly designed for people in relationships. It doesn't mean that it's easier for those who are, but it can feel othering for those who aren't. I cannot tell you how much I appreciate it when a coupled-up friend has the humility to acknowledge this. Just as I hope your single friends are compassionate when you face challenges related to being in a couple (fights, sex lulls, difficult in-laws etc.), you should do the same when imagining the single experience. Because that's all empathy actually is – really listening to someone, then using your imagination to put yourself in their position.

The other day I received a voice note from a best friend who has lived with her boyfriend for years and years. She was furious as a single friend of hers was looking for somewhere to live on her own in London and she soon realized her salary wouldn't even cover a studio flat in Zone 4. 'She's 37 and she's going to have to live with random people from a website just because she doesn't have a boyfriend,' she bellowed with fury. 'It's so UNFAIR.'

Some other quick tips: being single and sick and living on your own can be horribly lonely – when she is ill, don't ask her if there's anything you can do, just go round with some soup. If you don't want to go out on a Saturday night (which is totally fair), let her go out with her single friends and see her on a weeknight. Don't tell your boyfriend things your single friends have told you in confidence, it's an enormous betrayal of trust. Bad times are bad for everyone but good times are hard when you've got no one to celebrate with, so make sure someone's celebrating with her. Check if she has someone to have dinner with on her birthday, especially if her family live far away.

There are grown-up things that feel overwhelming when you don't have a partner: moving house, taking care of a relative, undergoing a serious medical procedure. It's embarrassing to ask your friends to help, because it makes you feel like you don't have your shit together. Keep an eye out for these changes in her life and offer to help before she has to ask.

Dear Dolly: 'My best friend is trying to get pregnant and has said our friendship will have to change because I drink too much'

My best friend is trying to get pregnant and has recently told me our friendship will have to change because of it, mainly because she thinks that I drink too much. We haven't spoken since, and I don't know what to do. I'm supportive of her plans, but hurt that she thinks I have to change.

I don't know how much you drink and I don't know if drinking negatively affects your life, so I can't agree or disagree with your friend. But you don't think alcohol is a problem and you haven't mentioned that any other friends agree with her. So, I'm going to work from the presumption that you are a person who enjoys too many pints on a Friday night, rather than too many bottles of Buckfast on a Monday morning. In which case, it's likely that this isn't so much about you, but more about her.

I don't think what you are describing is that unusual for a woman who is starting a family, it just sounds like your friend has articulated herself badly. Deciding to have a child is a primal desire, and primal desires can make us behave in uncharacteristic ways (my excuse for writing those love poems about Charlie from Busted all those years ago). I have known women who, while pregnant or trying to get pregnant, have decided to hunker down and keep themselves in an environment that is as safe and calm as possible. Often that means changing their habits, and with those changes comes distance from certain friends. It's an instinct for self-protection, and I understand it. But I also understand that it hurts to be on the receiving end – to feel as if the way you happily live your life might repulse or even endanger someone (although I have the impression from friends that an afternoon glass of wine with a mate was one of the perks of the otherwise fairly full-on experience of maternity leave). You have to try hard not to personalize her words, and you must have an honest conversation with her.

It is possible that when she says she is concerned about your drinking, what she means is that she is concerned about her own drinking when she is around you. Perhaps she doesn't want to spend time with you because she associates your time together with alcohol, which is something she wants to leave behind. If that's the case, you can and should be sensitive to that. But she needs to find a way of not placing the responsibility for her relationship with booze on you. It's not fair that you should become her unofficial representative of The Bad Things, and therefore someone to avoid.

There's also a huge difference between telling you that your friendship has to change and that you have to change. If, as she moves into this new phase of her life, she feels like she wants low-key, alcohol-free or cosy hangouts with you, I don't think that's unreasonable. I hardly think you're going to suggest to a pregnant woman or mother of a newborn that you catch up at a rave over a gram of ketamine. The '5 p.m. dinners at Giraffe' years of your friendship may well be officially open from this point. They're different, but they don't have to be any less loving – it's just what happens as you grow up. I'm sure you have other friends who still want to party with you, so you should go on nights out with them instead.

The other reason she may want you to change your lifestyle is to reinforce that her decision to have a baby is the right one. This is something you notice more and more as you get older – we want our friends to do what we're doing to reassure us that we're doing the right thing. But we have to resist that desire for uniformity. Not only does it offer zero proof that our decisions are right for us, but also friendships would be very boring if everyone we knew was living exactly the same type of life.

I think it's worth making it clear that you support this big, exciting change, while also acknowledging that she can't ask you to reconfigure your life to accommodate her personal choices. I hope that you would never ask that of her either. Women should be allowed to take their lives in whichever direction works for them, without ranking those lifestyles in order of importance.

Watching a best friend become a parent is a magical thing. It can open up a part of their personality that you've never seen before and it can also open up a new chapter of your friendship. It is an adjustment that takes mutual commitment, but it is patience and acceptance worth finding. There is no better investment than the time put into a friendship that will see you through your entire life. If she wants to cut out booze, good on her, but it's in her best interest not to cut out friendships too. A baby is a life-changing love, but it's not a best friend. She'll need a couple of those by her side for the next eighteen years.

Dear Dolly: 'My friend's husband propositioned me – should I tell her?'

I was recently propositioned by my friend's husband and I'm unsure if I should tell her. It happened when a group of friends came back to my place after a night at the pub. My friend's husband was there and had been in the house for about two minutes before he asked me if I wanted to f***. Shocked, mortified and disgusted, I kicked him out. Since then he has begged me not to mention it to his wife. I'm almost certain it was a booze-fuelled moment and he would never try it again. But what if he tries it with someone else? I want to tell her but I'm scared I'll lose her friendship. Help!

Oh God. The stuff of nightmares. Poor you. I am glad you're thinking carefully about your next steps as, personally, I don't think there is a clear-cut answer for this one. There are so many factors that should be considered before you speak to your friend or choose to keep quiet. My general rule is that romantic relationships are complex, private and mostly none of our business. So allow me to wade in with *all my opinions*.

There are a few questions you need to ask yourself. The first: how close are you to this friend? Not to get too primary-school playground about it, but is she:

a) A best friend?
b) A very close friend?
c) A close friend of a close friend?
d) A woman you've worked with for a year who feels like a close friend, whose Colin the Caterpillar birthday cake you were definitely in charge of, but when one or both of you leave the company you will probably never see again?
e) A woman you have a quarterly dinner with?
f) A woman you see at parties and say, 'We should have dinner' – but you never do?

Unless the answer is a, b or c, I wouldn't even think about telling her. Telling her will launch a grenade into her marriage, the effects of which she will feel for years – do you really want to be the grenade wielder? And if you're not that familiar with them as a couple, you don't have any means to contextualize his comment. Which leads me to my second question.

How drunk was this man? And have you seen him drink before? I'm not a keen defender of drunks (despite what you may have heard), but I also do not blanketly subscribe to the theory that in wine there is truth. I think this differs from person to person. In some situations the vino brings out a lot of veritas. It is why so many rows between best female friends happen at about 4 p.m. on a bank holiday Monday on a picnic blanket surrounded by thirty-three empty bottles of rosé. But some people act like a completely different person when they're drunk. They talk rubbish. They don't mean any of it. Is there a chance that his comment came from nothing and means nothing? Next slide, please.

What kind of man is he normally? What's he like when he's sober? Is he a good partner? Is he supportive? Is your friend happy? Do they seem to have a solid marriage? If, over the years, you've only ever seen him be a kind and loving husband, is it fair to potentially ruin their relationship over a drunken comment? Or do you think this drunken comment is exemplary of who he really is? Was the night you describe a slip of the tongue or a slipping of the mask?

The last of the questions. Would you consider speaking to him? If you're going to drive yourself mad with speculation, would it be better to talk to him directly to get your answers? Could you suggest a walk or meeting up for a coffee, looking him in the eye and trying to gauge whether he's telling the truth? This might not be right for your situation – it might make you feel uncomfortable, or like a betrayal of your friend, which I understand. But it could also be the only way you'll get your answers and know what to do from there. Whether you speak to him or not, I strongly advise keeping this to yourself or confiding in just one trustworthy friend. Or a national broadsheet agony aunt. You don't want her life to become gossip and it end up getting back to her.

As you rightfully acknowledge, there is a risk he might be unfaithful, and his advances towards you were an indicator of what's to come. In which case it is your responsibility to let your friend know. But even then the fallout probably won't be simple. She might choose to forgive him and you could perversely become the bad guy. She might break up with him but feel too humiliated to retain a friendship with you. Telling her might be the right thing to do, but it will take some courage and conviction. If you do choose to tell her, remember that while the truth will set you free, it will make a bit of a mess first.

Dear Dolly: 'My best friend is so tight-fisted when it comes to money'

I have a best friend of nine years. We have always got on so well. However, she is so tight-fisted when it comes to money. She earns significantly more than me and my other friends (I know this because she talks about money so often), but is never afraid to say when someone owes her some, no matter how small the amount. She's never the first one to get a round in, and if she can get away with not paying her way, she will. I do value her as a friend, but feel like this is really affecting our relationship. Should I confront her or, at the most extreme, cut all ties?

Ah. Tight mates. We've all got 'em. It is one of those downsides of growing up that you can't avoid. When you are teenagers, students or graduates, most people's relationships with money either don't exist or are easier to hide. But once everyone starts their careers, setting up homes and establishing lifestyles, there it is. Money. Talk of it, lack of it, desire for more, incompetence with it, frustration that some people have more than others. You discover the financial habits of your friends, and they are sometimes at odds with the rest of their personality. The ones who are generous with their time and love can be stingy with their cash. The mates who are normally uptight and cagey can be relaxed about sharing money. And it so often makes no mathematical sense – why is it that the one in the group on the lowest salary is the one who buys all the rounds? And the one who earns well is the one who sends everyone their online banking details five minutes after picking up a packet of Kettle Chips from the corner shop?

What you're talking about is a very specific frustration, where a person is happy to exploit the generosity of others without returning the courtesy. I understand how infuriating this is – not only does it bring on that hot, prickly skin feeling of unfairness, but it also makes you feel used. It's humiliating to feel as though someone is taking advantage of your goodwill, and it's very upsetting when that person is a best friend.

But I don't think she's trying to pull a fast one on you, and I don't think she's boasting about her finances to make you feel inadequate. Our relationship with money is circumstantial, but it is also personal, historical and deeply psychological. It is informed by the numbers in an account, but it's also informed by the way money was earned and lost and spent in the households in which we grew up. Or our sense of control, or lack of control, over the future. How we behave with money is so often governed by fear. I don't think your friend is mean, I think she's probably scared.

When someone talks about something all the time – whether it concerns them or not – it means it is a topic that terrorizes them to some degree. Money is a common one; the same can be said of people who constantly comment on weight. As annoying and upsetting as that can be for bystanders, it's worth trying to remember how exhausting it must be to be in their head. I think your friend feels panicked about money and can't help but let it distort her behaviour. When she counts how much she is owed and immediately asks for it back, that's panic. When she compulsively discloses her financial security, that's not showing off, that's panic. She's using you as a human repository for her money worries. She thinks that if she lists her financial fears and achievements, they're somehow safe.

I think you should have a conversation with her in which you ask about her relationship with money and encourage her to open up about any anxiety she might have. Tell her that you want a friendship in which you can both be open about money, but in a way that is also sensitive and respectful and without awkwardness.

Because it's a really special thing, to help each other out when one of you needs it. Give her an opportunity to see how she's messing up and give her a chance to correct it. Mistrust with money has the power to ruin friendships in adulthood, and I can't think of a more stupid reason to lose someone you love.

Dear Dolly: 'I'm 32 and single, and now my friends are having babies'

I'm 32 and longtime single, and friends often wring their hands at my bad choice of men, worrying about me living alone with no one around. All has been fine until recently, when all my married friends started announcing babies. Suddenly I can't stop crying when I'm alone. Do I have to accept that maybe this isn't going to happen? Or can I hold on for the guy and the baby?

I very nearly didn't reply to this letter. I really wanted to, because it is a worry that I hear about constantly and know very well. My reluctance to address it is that it concerns female fertility and therefore female bodies. And people have a lot of opinions on female bodies. So my first piece of advice is to ignore any advice that makes you feel anxious or ashamed. Don't read the comments on this column. Don't read articles that cite fertility 'facts' from studies that date from 150 years ago. Don't believe the pseudoscience about female biology that you hear anecdotally. The only person you should listen to when it comes to your body is yourself and your doctor.

I've always found that when I can't stop crying, it is an expression of frustration. And I think that is the correct word to describe what it is to be a single woman in her thirties who wants a family and can see no clear way of making it happen. It's frustrating not to know how or when you'll meet the right person. It's frustrating to feel as if there is rapidly dwindling time to get pregnant. Every woman I know in your position says the same thing: 'If only someone could guarantee that I will have a baby at some point in the future, I'd stop thinking about it.'

Yet that cannot be guaranteed to anyone, whether they are single or with the person with whom they want to have children. The best way to keep the odds on your side is to make sensible, logical decisions rather than panic-based ones. For starters, enough with the bad men, lady. They're a drain on your time and heart. And your time and love are precious, irrespective of whether you want children or not. If you don't know why you keep choosing them, go to therapy. Or if that's not possible, ask your friends who know and love you to give their insight.

There is also the option of egg-freezing, but this is a deeply personal choice, dependent on a number of factors. One woman I know has saved up to do it and is really excited at the prospect – she sees it as the best present she could give herself for a slightly increased sense of freedom. Another friend recently did a U-turn on the process. She realized that she was only doing it out of fear and she didn't want to spend all that money on something that represented her own negative thought spirals. Do some research and have a think about whether this might be right for you. Again, freezing or not freezing your eggs won't guarantee that you will or won't have a baby.

You should also seek out the stories of women who are a bit older than you and have chosen a less traditional path. Most of the women I see as mentors, whom I've worked for and collaborated with over the years, did not meet their husband at university, get married at 25 and have two children before they were 30. Some of them had children on their own through IVF, sperm donation or adoption. Some never had children and don't regret it at all. All of their stories serve as a reminder that there is more than one way to have a settled, peaceful home life.

One of these women is a director who had her children in her forties. 'Once you have babies, Dolly, life is only about babies for a while,' she said. I found this such a helpful reminder to inhabit the stage I'm at right now, and be grateful for what it is at this precise moment, rather than dwell on what it isn't. Instead of looking at your life and seeing the lack, look for the abundance. Free time? Go to the cinema in the afternoon. Money that doesn't have to go on childcare? Buy a stupidly gorgeous handbag. Flat that's all yours? Paint every room your favourite colour and fill the fridge with Aldi champagne and stinky cheese.

Finally, my most important piece of advice is to keep giving love to the women who have everything you want. Any time you feel jealous of your friends, make a promise to yourself to turn it into an act of love and it will neutralize any feelings of bitterness. Message your friend who is a new mum and ask for baby photos. Go round to see her, take the baby and let her have a nap. Find out what your pregnant friend is craving and send her a pack of it in the post. Keep putting love out into the world and it will come back to you in one way or another. That, I've learnt, is one of life's only guarantees.

Relationships

1. Dating
2. Friendship
3. (Relationships)
4. Family
5. Sex
6. Break-ups
   & Exes
7. Body & Soul

Dear Dolly: 'I checked my boyfriend's phone while he was sleeping – now I feel so guilty'

My boyfriend and I have been dating for just under a year. He is kind, funny and patient and often tells me how much he loves me. The other night, while he was sleeping, I got a horrible urge to look at his phone. I saw a few messages to girls that he had sent in the first few months of us dating, but nothing that really worried me. I stopped looking after about two minutes, but have felt immensely guilty ever since. I do trust him and feel so lucky to have him – why am I trying to sabotage that by going behind his back?

Ah. Checking the sleeping boyfriend's phone. One of those utterly inexcusable things that most people do at one point in their lives. Like not correcting the waiter who undercharges you. Or calling a hangover 'suspected norovirus' in an email written to your boss while stuffing an Egg McMuffin in your gob. A high-risk decision motivated by our weaknesses that leads to an inevitable feeling of guilt that is never worth it.

You don't need me to tell you that checking your boyfriend's phone is a bad idea. You already know that it's sneaky and disrespectful. And that, in a matter of seconds, it obliterates the precious and hard-earned trust between you both. I'm sorry that you're feeling so tormented by the fact you did it, but I think it's a positive thing that you're keen to understand this compulsion. I wouldn't confess to him – it will only cause unnecessary angst that is unwarranted if you vow to never do it again.

The most obvious reason for checking his phone is mistrust. You say your boyfriend has given you no reason to doubt his loyalty to you, but I wonder whether you've encountered cheaters elsewhere. Chances are you've known people who have been unfaithful: your friends, your friends' boyfriends or your ex-boyfriends. If you have ever been cheated on, the low-level suspicion that it will happen again is always with you. You watch whether your partner turns down their phone screen when they put it on the table. Or whether it's always on 'do not disturb' mode so they don't receive notifications. You check whether they're online on WhatsApp after midnight and, if they are, try to convince yourself that male friends chat late into the night (they don't). You look for these signs as a survival method – to make sure you never feel the humiliation of betrayal again.

But there's a difference between being cautious and being suspicious. And to predict the wrongdoings of someone you love by the actions of people who bear no resemblance to him isn't fair. Perhaps it's a man thing – maybe you're disappointed in men and they've lost your trust. I get it. Every time I open a newspaper another one has disappointed me. But to briefly borrow school-teacher speak: you don't want to punish the whole class because of the few who misbehaved and ruined it for everyone.

It is also possible that your urge to check his messages is self-sabotage driven by low self-esteem. Perhaps, on some level, you don't believe you're worthy of fidelity. If you think there might be something in this, it's important you recognize that that's mostly your issue to work through. Romantic partners should be aware of each other's insecurities and be sensitive to them. But it's not their job to solve them. They can't. If you feel you're undeserving of adoration and commitment, it won't matter how many times your boyfriend tells you he loves you and will be faithful to you. You'll still suspect otherwise. You need to work out where that fear comes from and understand its irrationality.

Mostly, I think the urge to check a sleeping boyfriend's phone is a desire for control. There is so much said about the joys of falling in love, but I don't think enough is articulated about how terrifying it is. You hand over your heart and happiness to someone. You give them your body, your secrets, your weekends, your thoughts, your brain space, your future plans, your home, your keys, your friendship group, your family. I've said it before in this column, and I'll keep saying it: love is high-risk. Always. In so many ways. Sure, they might cheat, but they also might die. Have you thought about that? Or they might be a con artist. If you're worried your boyfriend might have an affair, you might as well also worry that he has a secret family in a neighbouring county.

Loving someone is not an act of control, it's an act of surrender. You can make careful considerations about who you choose to merge your life with, but from there you have to let go. The alternatives are to choose to be on your own (makes a lot of sense) or to be with someone whose infidelity you wouldn't care about, so you feel totally safe (miserable). You have to surrender to the unknown variables of another human. Know them, trust them and hope for the best.

Dear Dolly: 'My good friend recently confessed his feelings for me. Can you learn to fancy someone?'

My good friend recently confessed his feelings for me. He is intelligent, funny, hard-working and well dressed. The issue is I do not fancy him. I'm 29 and broke up with my ex of four years because he was fundamentally an unkind person. In movies I'm aware of the trope to 'get with the good guy who actually cares about you'. But I don't want to mess my friend around when I know I'm really not attracted to him. Can you learn to fancy someone?

OK, so I know there are lots of people who will disagree with me, and I know that anecdotally there are many, many examples that will disprove my theory and you should, of course, listen to them. But, first and foremost, I am going to speak from my own experience. No, you cannot learn to fancy someone.

I've seen loads of successful relationships form with a slow-burn attraction, and I think there's a real case to be made for incremental seduction. If we're really honest with ourselves, we all think we're going to lock eyes with someone across a crowded room and be struck with Cupid's sudden arrow or the thunderbolt recognition that a total stranger is going to become a spouse. Deep down I still think that's how it's going to happen for me and everyone single who I know and love. But, particularly as we get older, those love-at-first-sight stories become less and less common for a reason.

These days I'm much more likely to hear about relationships that began as a friendship or in a work environment or were initially a bit stop-start. Perhaps, as we get older and wiser and more cautious, we want to feel safe with someone before we fall in love with them. Maybe we lose faith in our own instincts – we learn that desiring someone so much that you want to rip off their clothes and maybe their skin and climb inside their body and zip it back up and live in their heart may not *necessarily* lead to the most healthy and functional long-term relationship (who knew?). Slow-burn attraction is good because it means you've got somewhere to go together – if you're super-intense from day one, it's hard to keep up.

Slow-burn attraction is still attraction, though. Initially it might not be sexual, or it might creep up on you or take a while for you to find the right language to understand it, but it always begins with some sort of magnetism between two people. You can't create that if it's not there. If you have known this friend for a long time and so far you've never felt any connection beyond a platonic one, I don't think it's going to happen now.

I have heard that you can have a 'love at first sight' moment with someone you've known for a long time and that you can, apparently, 'suddenly' realize you are in love with them. It happened to Monica and Chandler and Harry and Sally, after all. Maybe you're waiting for that moment with him. But again (sorry!), personally I have never found this to be the case. I don't think this really happens outside of films and TV, where the plots are decided by writers who need old friends 'suddenly' to fall in love for a satisfying third and final act. Whenever I have tried to escalate a friendship into something romantic just because we already get on and I know they're a nice person, it hasn't felt natural and it hasn't ended well.

When you come out of a relationship that caused heartbreak, often an overcorrection occurs with the next person you choose as a partner. You go for the absolute opposite of the last person you loved in the hope that it will protect you from replicating the same ending. This is especially common if you've dated someone who has been cruel. Looking out for kindness in a partner is a good idea, but kindness cannot replace attraction. They've got to be kind *and* you've got to want to kiss them. That is not a huge ask. I know you're probably still wounded and jaded having been treated badly by your ex, but hot, kind people are out there, I promise. The options for men aren't just fit and mean or kind and sexless.

And obsessing over who you 'should' be with is always a bad idea. When looking for a potential partner, it's good to think about compatible characteristics and what you're not willing to compromise on, but eliminating things you're attracted to like you're on a diet plan is not going to work. You can't date someone as an exercise of self-improvement, particularly when you know how much he likes you. Don't make him an experiment that's destined to fail. You can't think your way into a life (or even just a bed) with someone. Attraction doesn't only happen with your head, it happens with your heart and soul and . . . loins.

Dear Dolly: 'My boyfriend's parents don't like me. How can I win them over?'

I have recently moved in with my boyfriend, and we are really happy together. However, his parents are clearly struggling with the fact he has moved out (NB: he's in his mid-twenties) and have made it apparent that they do not like me. They seem to view me as the woman who took their son away. How do I win them over? I don't feel like I've done anything wrong, but I also don't want my boyfriend to suffer in the middle of this bizarre custody battle. What do I do?

One of the hardest things about being mature (other than no longer spending entire afternoons doing prank calls to boys on your mum's landline) is acknowledging when you have privilege in a situation, even when you feel entirely disempowered. I know that this feels humiliating – like you're being isolated by a gang. And I understand why you have that sense of being in a custody battle. But you're not. Your boyfriend has chosen to share his life and home with you. You are his new family, you are his new future. Therefore I'm afraid you're going to have to act with the grace and class of someone with the upper hand. I know. It's gutting.

If your boyfriend lived with his parents until his mid-twenties, they are obviously a very close unit. With my rose-tinted glasses on, I can see this is a good thing – it's lovely to settle down with someone who values family so highly. The downside is that these units are often hard to infiltrate, with their nicknames and their in-jokes and their weird traditions (who does crackers on *Christmas Eve*, for God's sake?).

So the key is not to try to break your way in, because you might never get full access. These best-friend-families are rarely recruiting for members – if they're looking for anything it's normally admiring spectators. You need to find a way of being around them that makes you feel included in the social situation, while making it clear to them that you don't need to be included in their family.

The way to do this is by showing (but not explaining) that you are in no way a threat – that the relationship you and your boyfriend have is incomparable to the one he has with them. This is a particularly important strategy to take with his mum, because men's relationships with their mothers are usually – not to generalize – demented.

There are subtle things you can do to indicate your respect for her without spelling it out in a way that is uncomfortable or mawkish. You could ask her for advice for a birthday present for him. Or, next time she is at the flat, you could ask for her opinion on something in the home. Request the recipe for a meal she cooked that you enjoyed.

It's not about being manipulative, it's about being sensitive. Diplomacy is a hugely underrated social skill and one that doesn't take huge amounts of effort. You just have to be aware of people's insecurities and gently try to balance the conversation or dynamics of the room until they feel comfortable. It's important to do all of this without being smarmy – don't overcompliment or overenthuse. People can always tell when someone is trying too hard and it immediately engenders mistrust.

It does take a bit of thought and work, but from my experience that's what's required when you merge disparate families through a romantic relationship. It can be difficult and complicated – there can be clashes and incompatibilities. Be reassured that this is a very common problem. It's rare to meet someone who had an entirely stress-free transition into their family of in-laws.

And try not to take it personally. I'm sure they would have made life awkward for any woman who came into his life in a long-term relationship. They might not even know that they're being difficult – perhaps they're just overwhelmed with loss, because they find themselves in a house without the boy who has lived in it for twenty-five years. Perhaps they're not even aware that this is manifesting as hostility towards you.

If this continues and it makes you unhappy, I think you should talk to him about it. Tell him that you feel like his family are struggling with the fact you are in his life and that you'd like to rectify it. Ask for his advice on how the situation could be made easier for everyone. Once again diplomacy is crucial here.

Whatever you do, don't slag off his mum and dad. Don't give any opinion on their personalities. Save all those observations for WhatsApp conversations with your best friends. We all know the inexplicable rule of families: we're allowed to say whatever we like about our own one, but woe betide anyone who expresses a similar opinion. Be patient. These relationships take time. If you're in it for the long haul with this man, you're in it for the long haul with them too.

Dear Dolly: 'My boyfriend is sweet and my best friend, but he doesn't intellectually stimulate me'

My boyfriend of almost two years is sweet, generous and my best friend, but he doesn't intellectually stimulate me. Our conversations lack depth and I often feel like we haven't really engaged each other. My heart sinks every time he doesn't catch my jokes. He has no inferiority complex, and constantly showers me with praise for my accomplishments, but it feels lonely up there without him. Do I continue and try to bridge our differences?

My mum and dad have been married for more than thirty years and they're one of the happiest couples I know. They're always laughing, they're affectionate with each other. But there's one great mystery of their relationship: their minds are entirely incompatible. My mum is an obsessive reader, my dad has only ever read one book (Michael Heseltine's autobiography). My mum loves museums, my dad hates them. They are at opposite ends of the political spectrum.

Over the years I've studied these differences, trying to work out how this cerebral chasm has not divided them. What I have finally deduced is that while they intellectually clash, they are spiritually matched. They find the same things funny, they find the same things moving. They react to other humans similarly. They want the same sort of relationship and family life. They're twins of the soul, if not twins of the brain.

I think that's the thing that really matters in a romantic relationship. You can outsource intellectual companionship to others. You can find fellow enthusiasts in online forums or at conferences or events. You can have friendships for discussing books and politics and ideas. Lots of couples have different interests and it shouldn't cause anxiety. So I wonder if what you're talking about is a spiritual incompatibility as well as an intellectual one. And I wonder if, when you say he is sweet and that he praises your accomplishments, what you mean is he adores you.

On the one hand I see the appeal of a relationship being founded on ease, comfort and one-sided worship. Love should feel uncomplicated and without huge stress. But an uncomplicated relationship doesn't have to mean an unstimulating one, a stress-free relationship doesn't mean it shouldn't challenge you. When we love one another, we learn from one another. That doesn't mean dating someone who lectures you on Marxism or Milton's poetry (heaven preserve us), but it does mean having mutual respect and interest in each other and how you view the world.

And as nice as it is to be adored, it's so, so fun to adore. Being entertained, beguiled or obsessed by the way someone thinks and communicates is an eternal pleasure. And I think most people who have experienced constant one-way devotion in a relationship will admit that the reality of it is not as enjoyable as imagined and the novelty wears off. Having someone hang on your every word is only really exciting if you want to hang on every word of theirs too.

I don't know your relationship history, so it's possible that you have an unrealistic standard for intellectualism – that your interests are esoteric or disparate and so are hard to match precisely. (I once gently had to tell a male friend he was never going to find a woman who was as clued-up as him on both the writings of Tolstoy and Jeremy Beadle's TV shows.) I also don't know what you're looking for in love. If you want something casual or slow moving, there's no harm in staying in the relationship a little longer to see how it develops. If you want to be with someone long-term and have a family, you need to examine how much you truly love hanging out with him. When two of my friends moved to the remote countryside with their newborn, the husband gave me some advice on finding a partner for which I'm forever grateful. 'There are a lot of long, dark nights, Dolly,' he told me, solemn and sleep-deprived. 'Make sure you marry someone you can have a great conversation with.'

I suppose I'm wary of my own advice in this instance because I have always been a defender of asking a lot from life. You (allegedly) only get one. And it is famously over before you know it. I have always thought that great love can coexist with great friendship, solid teamwork, physical attraction and lots of laughter. I was privileged enough to grow up in a household where that was a reality. But I also know that you can't get everything from a partner and that perfectionism is not only fruitless but often hypocritical.

I think you really need to interrogate what's important to you in a relationship (it may be different to everyone else you know, and that's fine). Work out what is non-negotiable and what you're willing to relinquish. You usually have to relinquish something. But it might not be this.

Dear Dolly: 'My husband is in his mid-forties and is rapidly turning into his dad'

My husband is in his mid-forties and is rapidly becoming his dad. He grumbles about minor things, and has an elderly posture, a lack of ambition and frequent fatigue, even choosing gardening as his next hobby. His dad is sweet, but that's not what I've chosen my spouse for. It irritates me a lot, as I'm still keen to enjoy life to the full. I understand that we all tend to become copies of our parents as we age, but now seems too early for me. What should I do?

There are a lot of things I want to say in response to your problem, but I'm aware that when I broadly ruminate on the characteristics of men, they can get upset. And fair enough. So I thought I'd weave the counter-arguments from an imagined middle-aged, Hampshire-based man into my answer. We will call him Peter. Let's get going.

Peter: Why are people looking to YOU for advice, you silly –
We haven't even started yet, fella! Hold on.

Peter: Hmmph.

I don't think this is an unusual worry. I've known many women who have approached middle or later life with their male partner and felt their respective energies and interests diverge. My theory is that women are more likely to mellow as they age and men are more likely to harden, because being a young woman is full of anxieties that slowly melt away as you get older.

Peter: This is why I hate feminism. Stop whingeing! Young women have NOT had a hard time.

I think they have, Peter! Fear of male violence, fear of accidental pregnancy, unequal work opportunities, fertility stress, impossible beauty standards, balancing new motherhood with a career. The first 45 years of a woman's life and the choices she makes are under enormous pressure and scrutiny. I can understand why most women I've encountered over the age of 50 say they've finally found the confidence and serenity they wish they'd had when they were 20.

Men, on the other hand, are encouraged to thrive when they're young and enjoy every moment of their virility. Just as so many women speak of the relief of unburdening themselves of youth, I understand why so many men are terrified of losing it. I think this fear is often misunderstood, so instead all we see is a grumpy older man. But I don't think most grumpy older men are being difficult, rather a culture of toxic masculinity means they're petrified of losing their power and relevance.

I think you need to dig a little deeper into his new habits and personality developments and work out what the cause might be. Have a conversation with your husband in which you ask him lots of questions that invite him to reflect on why his ambition and enthusiasm are waning. It is likely that the reasons are much more complex than him being tired or bad-tempered or turning into his dad – they could be emotional or existential. And talking about it might help.

Peter: HANG ON. Wanting to work diligently on a herbaceous border has NOTHING to do with our fear of ageing and death.

I'm loath to say that Peter does have a point. I think you have to find a way of separating these different behaviours and working out which ones are indicative of apathy and which are just someone getting older. Humans are not only allowed to change, they're supposed to change. It's one of the risks of committing to a long-term relationship – we also have to commit to the unpredictable future versions of a person. I think what is upsetting you is a fear that his spirit has altered, his excitement and appetite for life are diminishing. It must be a horrible thought, because those are the things that make you fall in love with someone. But it's possible for him to retain his enthusiasm for life while slowing down his lifestyle.

Peter: She wants a FANTASY MARRIAGE.

Just getting to that, Peter. If you do decide to have an honest conversation with your husband, make some specific and reasonable requests. Tell him what would put your mind at rest while also being willing to compromise. Perhaps you could let go of the gardening if he agreed to go out more and do things together. Maybe you'd allow for a little grumbling if he also talked about what's gone right in his day. He can't fix what he doesn't know is a problem, so I think it's only fair that you give him a chance to meet you in the middle.

And don't panic. I think this is a really normal part of spending a life with someone. New incompatibilities can appear in every decade and it doesn't mean disaster. It just means you have to do a bit of talking and thinking to help you return to each other.

Peter: Honestly, I think she's lucky she has a husband.

All right now.

Peter: And if you'd listen to some of your own advice you're so happy to dish out, maybe YOU'D have a husband.

Thank you, Peter.

Dear Dolly: 'I dated my new boyfriend's friend before I met him – but he doesn't know'

I have started dating a guy I met on Hinge who is really nice and a real gentleman. After a few dates I realized that one of his close friends is a guy who I went on a date with last year but have occasionally since sent risqué texts back and forth with. Do I bring up the fact I dated his friend or wait for it to come up in conversation? I am also mortified at my error in judgement – I sent the friend risqué photos that he might have saved. I am so worried that my boyfriend will think differently of me and end things. It seems unlucky that out of the millions of men in London I happen to stumble on two who are friends. My anxiety has become so bad that every time the guy I'm dating hasn't replied to me I assume he has found out and he's ghosting me.

There are about four million men in London. I would estimate, with some very quick research, that about one million of them are single. Of that one million, I think about 300,000 say they're single, but they're not single and actually have been 'casually seeing' a nice, cavapoo-owning woman called Sophie for eighteen months; 150,000 of them will be out of your age bracket; 100,000 will say things are 'too hectic at work' to text you back, but find the time to post Elon Musk memes on Instagram Stories. About seventy-five of them won't be on dating apps. Basically what I'm saying is that leaves about fifty men to date, so I don't think the odds of accidentally dating two friends are that crazy.

When I read your letter my overwhelming urge is to find you and give you a very very very big hug. Because all I can see in every one of your sentences is shame. Shame for your former single life, for dating, for being sexual, shame for your secret and shame for who you think you are. It is something I, along with every woman I know, have felt. It begins in girlhood and lives deep within us. It grows in small moments – when a one-night stand spreads a rumour about you, when a catcaller calls you a slut, when your parents let your brother's girlfriend share a bed with him when he visits home but your boyfriend is banished to the guest room. And shame grows in daily collective experiences of womanhood too – when you have to justify taking the morning-after pill. When you can't find menstrual products that aren't heavily scented with perfume. When legislation threatens to take away decision-making about your own body.

So many women I know feel shame. Hidden and historic, until it comes out in the strangest ways as we get older. Your fear of your boyfriend leaving you is a fear that he will think you are promiscuous. But why is that a responsibility you should have to carry? You are a single person who had a sexual connection with another single person. It was consensual and, I'm sure at some point, brought you pleasure. You didn't know your boyfriend even existed. You've done nothing wrong.

I often look to men in the public eye for inspiration on how to live without shame. The married political figure whose role is under intense scrutiny yet apparently still has the time for several girlfriends. The millionaire who was unapologetic about his S&M orgy when it ended up in a newspaper. The fraudster stockbroker who went to jail before Leonardo DiCaprio played him in a film about his career. Honestly, it fills me with both bewilderment and awe. Imagine having that much faith in your own inherent goodness. Imagine being *that* sure you were never going to get found out. *Imagine it.* I still find myself occasionally unable to sleep when I think about a man I sent flirty texts to ten years ago who had a girlfriend. You should not be living in fear. You shouldn't feel like you're on the run. I'll say it again: you've done nothing wrong. I know you must feel like his friend has a piece of you – like he has stolen something from you that shouldn't be his. But if he's a normal human he will know the silent pact that's agreed when two people exchange sexy texts or photos, which is that it's private and specific to its context.

You have nothing to be ashamed of. At worst it is very awkward. But that's all. You're an adult, so is your boyfriend, so is his friend – you all have a history, you can all move past awkwardness. And if he can't, he's not the sort of man you'd want to be with anyway.

The best way to deal with shame is to heave it out of yourself like that yoga mat you keep buried at the back of the cupboard. Tell him. Bring it into the light and you'll realize there was nothing to hide. It doesn't matter how perfect you try to be, there's no circumventing the random shambles of life – the strange connections, the ghosts of yesteryear, the surprising twists. So you may as well laugh about them, preferably with the people you love.

Dear Dolly: 'My boyfriend relies on me financially and it's starting to bug me'

My boyfriend says he 'wants a job and not a career'. He relies on me financially and it's starting to bug me. I want him to be happy, but I also want him to have something to bring to the table. What should I do?

We need to dismantle this question, because it has as many parts as an Ikea Billy bookcase. I'm not sure which components are yours and which are his and which of them hinge together. And I think it's important you consider all of them. So, here goes.

Wanting a job and not a career is a perfectly reasonable wish. Honestly, I think it's quite commendable. I think a lot of us feel like we're locked into a cult of career and we don't know who we would be if we left. Career-building can become an obsession – it can steal your time, sleep, interests and relationships. And, most crucially, it can all fall apart. Businesses close, people get sacked, whole industries can go under with the twists and turns of an ever-changing society. I completely understand why some people want work to be something they only think about between the hours of nine and five for five days a week. I don't think a person needs to be professionally ambitious to be impressive and interesting. I don't think the hours spent in an office or studio or study are more important than the ones spent at home, travelling, or in pubs and parks. I don't think being a good boss or colleague is more important than being a good friend or family member. And I don't think anyone should pressure themselves into having an extraordinary work life if they don't want one.

However, that might not be appealing to you in a romantic partner. And that's also completely fine. You might be someone who is very career-focused and you might want a boyfriend who can match that drive. Perhaps that is just what you find attractive. If that's the case you need to break up with this man because he has been explicit about not only who he is but that he is content with his choices. He should be with someone who can accept him in his entirety, and you should accept who you are too.

Now, the money. Wanting a job rather than a career might mean that he doesn't have ambitions to earn an above-average salary. Again, totally understandable. But that doesn't mean that he should rely on your work and earnings to give him a lifestyle that he wants. If this is the case you have every right to feel a bit annoyed. But my next question is: is he actually asking you for money? Or is this in fact a pressure you're putting on him? Are you jointly spending money on things he can't afford, such as rent, holidays or groceries? Have you ever asked him what he can comfortably give to fund your life together? If it's less than you'd like, would you be happy to adjust your choices to reduce your joint outgoings, or would you prefer to fill the deficit with your own cash? Or would you prefer not to think about any of these things and instead date someone who earns the same amount of money as you?

It's not unusual for one member of a couple to earn significantly more than the other. I know plenty who have made it work, but never without boundaries, acceptance and a lot of communication. (I know that probably sounds tiring, that word makes me feel tired just looking at it.) I think there are two factors that potentially make it more challenging: the first, if the primary earner is a woman. Traditionally it has always been the other way around and navigating your way through compromised male pride can be a real drag, not to mention working out the specifics of maternity leave and childcare if you decide you want to have a baby. The second is if the lesser-paid half has no interest in their own career. I think it's easier to support a partner on account of a job that they're devoted to, that makes them happy and happens to pay less. If you were to continue with this financial dynamic, you would have to be willing to accept that not being devoted to his job is the thing that makes him happy.

I've always thought that we rely far too much on shared interests for romantic compatibility. It's one of the reasons dating profiles can be so misleading – sure, it's great that you both love short-haired cats and the albums of Elbow, but what does that really predict about your life together? I think we can easily overlook so many important factors when picking a long-term partner. One of them is the question of how important money is to both parties. I'm sorry to have answered your dilemma with more questions than you initially posed, but I think they're worth thinking about if you want a future with him.

Dear Dolly: 'Do you believe in right person, wrong time?'

Do you believe in right person, wrong time? I am in my early twenties and feel I have found the person I am supposed to be with. They say when you know, you know, and I really think I know. He feels the same. However, right now we have no time to see each other because of our careers. How are you supposed to let go when it feels so right and nothing has gone wrong? Do I wait?

Your problem is one I have been thinking about a lot over the past few years. Obviously I don't have the answer. But, like any good agony aunt, I have a much clearer and more certain perspective on your dilemma than I do on my own. Maybe I should write in to myself. No, too mad even for me.

Anyway. I've flip-flopped on this relationship conundrum for a long time. Yes, I do believe in right person, wrong time. But I also think that a 'wrong time' is nearly always a self-constructed limitation. When someone says they can't be with someone because it's 'the wrong time', (mostly) they believe what they're saying – I've been that person many a time. And that belief is hugely frustrating and saddening, but I don't think it's strictly true. Our relationship schedules aren't dictated by some

99

greater power. We don't get a calendar issued to us by a relationship boss that tells us which years or months we have to be single or have to be committed to someone. We have full control of our own timing if we meet someone we like who also wants to be with us. It might not be what we expected, it might take more thought to make it work, but we *are* in charge of our own decisions when it comes to love.

So why are we so preoccupied with this idea of there being a perfect time to be in a relationship? I think, first, it's about our own personal concept of freedom. Some people instinctively associate being single with being free – having the time and permission to go on adventures or have lots of experiences or focus on building a career. I am one of these people. For others, commitment is their meaning of freedom. They see the great adventure of life as merging lives with another and having lots of experiences together. I know a lot of serial monogamists with enormous careers who credit their success on having been in a serious relationship for their twenties. 'I didn't have to waste time worrying about dating,' one of them once said to me.

I also think our obsession with this nebulous thing called 'timing' is to do with our equation of a successful relationship with an eternal one. If we meet someone who feels right for us, we have been told it means we should be with them until the day we die. And if we aren't with them for all that time, then our initial instinct that they were right for us was incorrect. I think this is – if I may speak plainly – batshit crazy. If this is how we view relationships, how is anyone ever going to commit to anyone in their twenties? Or thirties, even? It's way too much pressure to put on ourselves.

Maybe you and this guy are meant to be with each other for a year, or five years, or a handful of months. That's fine! That can still be a successful relationship! You will still have an opportunity to grow together, to enrich each other and teach each other and make some beautiful (or even just fun) memories together. You don't have to wait for a precise moment when you know you will only be with each other for ever and ever, because otherwise you may not ever be with each other. Ask yourself which is the greater loss: having tried to be with someone you deem to be perfect and at some point breaking up or never having tried to be with them at all?

I understand your anxieties about career. I've always found that the most productive and focused times professionally have been when I am single – it is one of the reasons I have been single for a long time. But more recently I've realized that some of the most energized and inspired times in my career have been when I'm in love. Solitude has benefited my work enormously, but I now know the right partner does as well. Being single might be just what you need at this time in your life, but the support and love of this man could be too. I suppose you won't know until you try.

I'm aware I'm only 33 with a lot of living and loving and lessons ahead of me, but there's something I already know for definite: it's really, really rare to find someone whose company you can't get enough of. It's not often that you meet someone you completely adore. Gorgeous, kind, silly, sexy, giggling-when-the-lights-are-out love is not an easy thing to find. My advice is to try to enjoy it when it comes your way, however long it may last.

Dear Dolly: 'I've discovered my boyfriend is on a dating app'

Last week a friend of a friend messaged me to tell me that she had found my boyfriend on a dating app. She screen-grabbed his profile, and my heart dropped when I saw a photo I had taken of him. I asked him about it and he said he was embarrassed (damn right) and upset. He said it was a 'blip' and thinks he did it for validation. I asked to see the app and scrolled through messages – he hadn't answered any of them, which somehow makes it better but it's still so not OK! We have been together for a little more than two years and live together. Do I give him another chance or do I leave?

I've seen these men out and about over my years on dating apps. The faces that look familiar and only on closer inspection do I recognize as the boyfriend of someone I know or an old colleague who is meant to be married. Like your friend's friend, I usually assume it's an old profile. But I've also heard lots of stories exactly like your own. I was on a dating app that has an 'I'm just here for friends' function that displays on your profile, which I like to call the 'I don't want my wife's mates to tell her I'm on here' function. I'm always staggered that they think they'll get away with it. Be warned: if friends of your girlfriend see you (and they will – every person who is single is on a dating app now), there is no woman more loyal than the friend of a woman scorned.

Before I give you my thoughts, I want to make something perfectly clear: the only person who can decide if this is acceptable is you. I used to be highly judgemental about what couples allow or don't allow within their relationship, but increasingly I understand that every person has their individual limits. Your fuse is its own length, decided by your own experiences and personality. It's totally up to you whether you forgive him or not, and you shouldn't let other people's judgements be the things that dictate your choice. You know him better than your friends, and if you believe his reasons and you feel like it won't happen again and you really want to stay with him, then you should follow that instinct.

When I first read your letter I wondered what the cause of your boyfriend's self-proclaimed 'blip' might be. Is he very young and unsure whether he's ready for a serious relationship? Are you his first girlfriend? Is he in his mid-thirties and at that bit that so many men get to where they become terrified of life's next stage of commitments? Have you had a recent experience that made him feel unimportant or emasculated? None of these are excuses for setting up a dating profile, but I'm just trying to understand what he thinks his moment of crisis was.

Maybe it really was as simple as a need for validation. I do think the fact he didn't engage in conversations with his matches is an important detail. Dating apps were designed to feel like a game and that's exactly how a lot of people use them. They acquire matches with other humans like Mario collecting coins in *Kart* – the higher the acquisition, the closer they get to winning. Winning what? Not a partner but the reassurance that they are desirable. If your boyfriend really is this unsure of himself and can't find his sense of security and confidence within a loving relationship, I feel very sorry for him. And whether you want to support him through those insecurities is up to you.

What I will say is: if this is true, it's very early on in a relationship for him to feel so destabilized. You haven't mentioned that you two have faced any difficulties, so I worry that the relationship in a state of calm still caused him to 'need validation' elsewhere. What happens if you start a family and your attention is diverted off him and on to a baby for a while? What happens if he loses his job and you get a promotion? What happens when any of life's stresses and misfortunes are thrown at you individually or together in the future – will he return to 'needing validation' in those moments of uncertainty?

And the other thing to ask yourself beyond the ethics of his behaviour is the attractiveness of it. Personally, there's nothing I find less hot than a shady fella. I have known (and put up with) a lot of them. These days my dream man is a man who wants to commit – it is the muscle tone I find sexiest. I want a man who doesn't hide his phone or have a secret online life or have one foot out the door of the relationship. I don't think that's a particularly lofty dream. And I don't think it's a lot to expect of your boyfriend.

Dear Dolly: 'We got together through an affair. When will we stop being judged?'

My partner and I got together through an affair, and now I'm ashamed of being happy. We met at work while we both were with our long-term partners. The way things went down got ugly, but we came out of it together and we are truly soulmates. We want to share our happiness with our friends and family, some of whom were connected to our past relationships, and are faced with the shame and judgement associated with getting together through an affair. This idea of 'having to lay low' and being 'respectful of the people who were hurt along the way' is in itself ruining our relationship. A few years have passed now. How long do we have to wait before we can show our love openly and freely, like other happy couples?

There was a time, when I was very young and very stupid, when I was spectacularly judgemental of those who had affairs. Maybe it's because I went to Sunday school until I was 13, where they had a pretty hard party line on all the coveting of the neighbour's wife stuff. Maybe it's because in 2004 I was meant to be revising for my GCSEs and all I can remember reading about was David

Beckham and Rebecca Loos. But I knew that people who cheated were indisputably bad people.

To state the obvious for a mo: sex outside of a monogamous relationship is not great behaviour. There have to be sanctions to protect the preciousness of promised fidelity, the consequences of which you and your partner are still experiencing. But I don't always think affairs are symptomatic of poor ethics.

Affairs normally hurt everyone involved – even the people who appear to have had the good time. I recently watched an interview with the friends of Nora Ephron and Carl Bernstein – the once-married couple who divorced when Ephron found out about Bernstein's affair while she was pregnant with their second child. She wrote a bestselling novel based on the experience that was turned into a film, and he was publicly hated and humiliated. 'In the long run it hurt him more than it hurt her,' they said.

I'm sure there are readers of this column who will be pearl-clutching at the suggestion that the people who conduct affairs deserve any empathy at all. And I understand that. But I also think it takes a sizeable lack of humility for someone to say they absolutely know that they are incapable of ever being unfaithful. Nearly every person I've known who has cheated on their partner was convinced that they were incapable of infidelity until it happened.

I'm sure for both of you, your affair and subsequent relationship have caused a great deal of pain to the people you left. I'm sure the experience has left them with anxieties that will have an effect on how they love for the rest of their lives. I feel very sorry for them. I also feel sorry for you and your partner. I'm sure you've felt a lot of shame and guilt in this process.

It's such a complicated thing to advise on, because I understand why people are hurt and angry at both of you and I also think you have a right to be happy. I think, somehow, you're going to have to accept validity in all of those stances. You have to let their residual pain and judgement exist and try to ignore it.

The fact is, life is unfair. I suppose that's a rather trite thing to say, isn't it? But I often think of this truism when it comes to unrequited love. People want to be with the wrong people – it's one of life's most common emotional injustices. Most of us will experience it at some point: the person who loves us is not the person we want to be with, or the person we want to be with is not the one who loves us. There's a reason why Shakespeare and Austen got so much material out of it.

Another truism: you only get one life. And while that doesn't mean we should behave recklessly with no regard for the feelings of others, it does mean we shouldn't stay in relationships that don't make us happy. If you believe the old adage that infidelity is just a symptom that something else is wrong in the marriage, then there's a strong chance that your respective relationships would have broken up for another reason further down the line.

'The heart is a very resilient little muscle.' That's a line from a film that I quote too much. But I find more truth in it with every year I get older. Loving someone and losing them is a fact of life. Some of us will grieve more than others, but all of us will have to learn to live with absence of some sort. Your exes (and their friends) may not ever get over what happened. And you probably won't ever be able to forget what you did to them. You can't eradicate the pain you've all felt, all you can do is learn from it and continue to live and love as truthfully as you can.

Family

1. Dating
2. Friendship
3. Relationships
4. 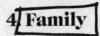 Family
5. Sex
6. Break-ups
   & Exes
7. Body & Soul

Dear Dolly: 'My kids are exhausted from meeting my latest flames'

I seem to have no luck in love. My three daughters, son and close friends tell me that they are suffering from 'girlfriend fatigue'. Apparently they are exhausted from meeting my latest flames. They claim there has been an endless stream of eminently suitable ladies, none of whom matches up to my exacting standards. Even in lockdown I've started seeing a fabulous lady who owns a trendy wine bar, but I remain confused.com when it comes to love. I'm now at a loss as to how to proceed and wonder if you would be so kind as to offer me a route map. I'm an attractive retired dentist (own hair and teeth), financially independent, very funny; I can sing but not dance.

Warm regards, Jim

I don't think anyone should come down too hard on you for this. There are far worse ways to conduct yourself in dating than being picky. It's better to be too exacting in your standards when looking for a partner than completely unselective. High self-esteem (with humility) is an underrated quality: if you can't believe you deserve happiness, who can? But then again, I'm not your daughter, and I don't have to meet an 'endless stream' of 'eminently suitable ladies' while you tell me you're 'confused. com', so I understand their frustrations. There is an internet phrase you may or may not be aware of: 'a messy bitch who lives for the drama' – a person who creates unnecessarily complicated situations for themselves. There may be a whiff of this about you, Jim.

Perfectionism is fascinating, as it is so often a counterproductive, even self-destructive, route to what we desire. And there are lots of different motivations. A reductive reading of your dilemma would be that you seek perfection because you yourself think you are perfect: that you have an inflated sense of your own qualities and therefore demand the same delusions of impossible excellence from a romantic partner. But I don't think that's what we're dealing with here. (Although, in the future, I'd avoid describing yourself as 'very funny' and let other people decide that for you. The more you insist on it, the less true it becomes to everyone who listens to you. Just a little something I've learnt on this journey we call life.)

I think it's likely that you think of yourself as a romantic. And romantics are, ironically, the worst culprits for being relationship-avoidant. This is for two reasons: the first being that committing to someone would mean they would have to call off the search for love, and nothing is more exciting for a romantic than longing. The second is that they spend a lot of time thinking about who their partner might be, so it's hard to find the 3D version that matches who they have invented in their mind. It's less about perfection and more about prescriptivism – they write their own version of how they think love is going to pan out, then they find it perplexing that no one seems to know the specific plot and characters other than them.

In short: you might be putting off the actualization of a relationship because the thought of it disappointing you is terrifying. I think that's an understandable fear. It's why perfectionism is often the reason cited for professional procrastination: better to put off the work and for it to be theoretically wonderful than deliver it and it be a letdown.

You've lived enough life by now to know that you can't select an array of random specifics that suit your whims and expect to find a human that replicates them entirely. That is not a suitable hobby for anyone other than 14-year-old girls casting spells to conjure their dream boyfriend by burning lists of adjectives over a makeshift bonfire in the garden. You can't summon someone who you've designed, because that doesn't allow for the unpredictable flaws of the people we end up loving. Fun people still have tempers. Bookish people can be ignorant. Really sexy people, I'm sorry to tell you, often leave discarded teabags in the sink. But you have to get stuck in to the whole person if you're ever going to experience any kind of real intimacy – you can't pick and choose the best bits. Someone recently said to me: 'When I spend time with my friends, I commit to the full experience of them.' I thought it was a lovely way of defining what acceptance means.

The other possibility is that you might not actually want a relationship. I'm sure you've thought about this, but people come up with all kinds of excuses for not finding a partner, because they think being without one isn't an option. It is an option. You have a life that's evidently already replete with love and company. You could fill your time with those people, in trendy wine bars or otherwise.

Think about the handful of attributes that you really value in a girlfriend above all else, then let go of all other expectations and allow yourself the fun of being surprised by someone. Be really honest with yourself about what's important and what's not – if you're expecting someone to accept all of you, you will have to show them the same courtesy.

Because, while I am sure you do have wonderful hair and teeth and a very impressive singing voice, you too will have your downsides. It's not pleasant to dwell on for too long, but there will be things about you that your friends and family have to endure when they commit to the full Jim experience. Things you might not even be aware of – things that make your friends sigh on the way home after a long dinner with you and say: 'Bloody hell, Jim was being very *Jim* tonight, wasn't he?' It's called being human. It's a gorgeous, shambolic humiliation and none of us gets it right. Come join us. You'll like it.

Dear Dolly: 'My mum has a fake news internet addiction and is embarrassing me beyond belief'

I adore my mum, but she has fallen into a fake-news-believing internet addiction. She posts constantly on Twitter and Facebook, embarrassing me and my siblings beyond belief. We have tried talking to her, but she only gets more stubborn and cross. She is a strong character with lots to say, and as much as I support that, it is hurting us a lot. Any advice?

There are few things as painful as watching your parents get something wrong. When our friends make arses of themselves it's funny. But there's something about your own mum or dad taking a public misstep that feels horrifying. The discomfort is twofold. We want to protect them from humiliation. And we feel inextricably, embarrassingly linked to their actions.

You are far from alone. I don't know anyone who would happily hand over their parents' social media accounts as a fair representation of who they are. Over the years we have all endured mums making their Facebook status the full name of their daughter's ex-boyfriend, thinking it was the search function. We've read the rambling, earnest tweets on Remembrance Sunday with a pixelated photo of a poppy field. We've had those chain emails from dads that begin 'FWD THIS TO EVERY1 YOU KNOW. 5G ROUTERS WILL EXPLODE ON MARCH 1ST'. We've all known what it is to go home for the weekend and find that a parent will barely look up from their iPad because they're so invested in the accumulation of pigs for their fantasy FarmVille smallholding.

A lot of boomers use the internet differently to us, and it's because they didn't grow up with it. We acquired the internet from childhood like a language – most of us are instinctively fluent in internet. I am reminded of this every time my mum checks her email and she goes into the Google search bar and writes 'check my googlemail inbox' and then clicks on the first result. 'You know you can just write gmail.com into the browser, Mum,' I tell her every time, inexplicably exasperated. 'It will take you straight to your emails. You don't have to search for it on Google.'

'I'm fine doing it this way,' she always replies.

It's a mistake to expect the same online behaviour from your parents that you'd expect from your friends. Your parents are always going to use the internet differently to you – they'll express themselves differently, they'll have a different audience and different types of interactions. You don't have to panic about people reading your mum's statuses and tweets and thinking she is an ambassador for your thoughts and tastes. Unless your mum is making statements that are hurtful or offensive (which it doesn't sound like she is – the content just sounds a bit nuts), I think you have to let her get on with it.

The internet can be unforgiving – a place of judgement and punishment. This is the occasional downside to an otherwise very good thing: that sensitivity is valued and monitored online. That said, I do think that most people allow for a Mum Metric – an acknowledgement that people over 60 may not be quite as effortlessly aware of the rules as we are. No one is going to click on your mum's social media pages and expect her to be as succinct as a viral comedian. Don't worry about her getting into trouble – it doesn't sound like she will. And if someone pulls her up on something she shares online, she sounds like she's more than capable of handling herself.

When people gravitate towards conspiracy as they get older, the culprit is normally fear. Fear of a world in which they feel confused or powerless. Fear of a world that they're leaving their children to live in one day. Fear of the unknown. Rather than scolding her, try to understand why she's chosen extreme theories to give her comfort during this time of uncertainty. And try to start conversations in which you share information with each other, rather than catch each other out. Facts are your friend – send her articles stuffed with them, and present them as something you think she'd enjoy, rather than as proof she is wrong.

And when you next find yourself frustrated by her, remember: she put up with you when you wore combat

trousers and thought Limp Bizkit were the greatest artists of our time. She thought your tastes and opinions
were wrong, yet she stuck around regardless. And one
day, as impossible as it might seem, your children or
nieces and nephews will be cringed out by your mere
existence. This mortification cycle is part of the circle
of life, my friend. We take turns to be embarrassed,
patiently trying to guide each other back in the right direction. I think it's part of the deal of love.

Dear Dolly: 'I love my older sister, but we have opposing views on politics'

My eldest sister and I have always been close, despite a ten-year age gap. However, a rift has begun to appear: we have opposing views on many political/social topics, me being the very liberal lefty and her being more conservative. I love her so much, but feel like I cannot remain quiet when she says certain things. How can I remain true to my values without losing her friendship?

I'm not sure I've ever before experienced a time in adulthood where morality is so conversationally unavoidable. For some years, in a period when relative peace coincided with youth, it seemed like my friends and I were all on the same page of General Ethics. And knowing that was enough. Most of us voted Labour and put tins in the food bank. We slagged off Margaret Thatcher, cried when Tony Benn died, stuck an EU flag in our window and boycotted palm oil until we realized it was used at Pret.

But more recently there is no avoiding the stuff that really matters when it comes to politics – the specific, the urgent and the uncomfortable. Whether it's discussions of pandemic control, or how racism exists in

systems from which many of us benefit. These are subjects that demand our time and honesty, rather than
broad theorizing. These are very human issues affecting
our daily lives, often in very personal ways.

I too would call myself a 'very liberal lefty' and reading those words in your letter made me trepidatious in
recognition. Because, while I know our intentions are
good, I think that that kind of self-identification can
encourage complacency. If we decided long ago that we
were on the side of the good guys, it might mean we
now avoid the brutal work of self-examination. When
we oppose someone's views, our immediate assumption
is probably that they're ignorant. When we point out the
mistakes of others, we could be resistant to inspecting
our own hypocrisies. And I think we are frightened of
being near the 'wrong' opinion, in case we catch it. It's
easy for 'very liberal lefties' to think of conservative
values like the plague – we don't want proximity to them
at risk of infection or a black cross on our door. I've
been guilty of all of the above, and I don't think any of
it is particularly liberal.

I say all this not to undermine how upsetting it is
when someone you love espouses opinions you detest.
But I wonder if you could see this as an opportunity,
personally and politically, rather than a barrier. A lot of
people hold right-wing opinions (let's not forget that
almost 74 million of them voted last month in the US).
Here's a chance to help understand why. The truly liberal
people I've met are not the ones who try to inform,

they're the ones who try to learn. They are sure of what they know to be true, yet flexible in their understanding of others.

There is a tendency to believe that we are the sum total of our political persuasion. I agree to a certain extent (particularly when those politics mobilize action), but as you and your sister demonstrate, opinions are not always hereditary. They can be formed by experiences. She may not have told you the origins of her beliefs – there might be a specific reason her views have intensified over time. Is she reacting against something or someone? Is she responding to something traumatic? Has she reached for this ideology as a solution because she feels misunderstood or ignored?

If you really feel like you cannot speak about politics without ending up in an argument, the only solution is to not talk about politics. This is an awkward tango, but one that has been danced by many family members in many living rooms for many, many years. Your unwillingness to remain silent in response to views that offend you is admirable, and not something you should change about yourself. You'll have to agree mutually to change the tenor of your relationship instead.

But first – talk. I know it's hard to remain patient when someone is speaking in a way you find abhorrent, but try to take the heat out of the debates. Do it away from onlookers, which can encourage rhetorical showboating. Tell her that you want to understand how she reached her stances – if you set that tone, it's likely she will show you the same courtesy and curiosity. When conservatives feel patronized by liberals, there's only one way they turn, and that's further right. Anything you want your sister to know will be more effectively received in calm, compassionate conversation – as, to paraphrase the US president-elect, opponents rather than enemies.

Dear Dolly: 'My daughter is 34 and single, and I'm worried she'll never meet someone'

My daughter is 34, attractive and has her own flat. She is successful in her career and is a lovely, kind person (my friends tell me this too). She has lots of friends who are mostly married or in relationships, but they all still involve her in social activities and she meets them frequently. She is also happy to travel solo and has been on many world trips with friends and alone. It might sound ridiculous, but I just feel very unhappy for her that she hasn't got somebody to share the travelling with, to hold her hand and cuddle up to after a bad day at work. She has had a few longish relationships but they haven't worked out, and I know she would like to settle down and eventually have a family like her brother. The worry is tearing me apart but I never show her. My friends are mostly not in the same situation so empathize but don't really understand how I feel. Please can you give me some wise words.

Mum! Lovely to hear from you.

No, joking aside, you have my sympathy. I still can't quite imagine what it's like to bring a teeny-tiny helpless creature into the world, care for it, raise it, watch it grow

into a fully formed human, and then let it just walk out
of the house and into the world aged 18, probably not
wearing a proper coat. I don't know how parents don't
stay up all night every night, worrying about their off-
spring at large. Do they know about all the things they
could be doing? Do they think about all the stuff they
could be sniffing or snorting? All the roads they're walking across without looking left then right then left again?
All the people who could be mocking them or taking
advantage of them or breaking their heart? Do parents
ever consider the instruments we use to scoop Nutella
out of the jar when none of our knives are clean? I'm
amazed you've got a good night's sleep in thirty-four
years, in all honesty.

I say all this not to concern you, but to remind you
that parental concern is one that is as much formed by
primal instinct as it is objective rationality. I am sure if
you met a 34-year-old woman of your daughter's descrip-
tion who wasn't your daughter, you would not think that
she was in need of your sleepless nights and worry.

Your daughter has time: 34 is young. People meet
their partners and start families at all different ages
depending on a number of factors, and there isn't a
superior timeline. When everyone around you happens
to be making exactly the same choices at exactly the
same time, it is tempting to believe that you're the one
getting it wrong, but – as clichéd as it might sound – it
really is only right for them. I imagine it's likely you met
someone and had children at a younger age, which might

be why you're feeling anxious that your daughter isn't doing the same. It is natural to want people to experience the things that have brought us happiness – but you're applying your own framework of desires to someone whose life trajectory is completely different to yours.

Falling in love and finding a compatible partner with whom to have children is determined by so many things, many of which are out of our control. It isn't something you can decide and schedule, and the people who view romantic partnerships that way – where the partner is a means to an end – don't end up in happy marriages.

And the truth is her attitude towards marriage and children is probably in a state of flux. I'm not sure when she told you she wanted a family, but it might have been in her twenties, when marriage was a notional idea of drinking a lot of buck's fizz in a marquee, and having a baby required a similar level of maintenance to watering an aspidistra. As a single woman so much can change when you watch your friends and siblings have children. It can deepen your desire for long-term love and a family, or it can heighten your fear; most confusingly, it can do both simultaneously. Have faith in her own instinctual judgement about what will work for her.

It's good that you haven't confided your worries in her. Trust me – she's aware of her aloneness, whether she's absolutely certain she wants a family or is still undecided. The world has been built for her to not forget about it. She's aware of it every time she watches a harmless lol-sy video of a hedgehog taking a bath and is greeted with a targeted YouTube ad for Clearblue pregnancy and ovulation tests. Continue to not mention it – no woman ever needs her mum to remind her of her biological clock. This is not something that's ever going to slip her mind.

What you should find most reassuring is that your daughter evidently has a very full life – you mention friends, a career, her own home, varied travel. You describe someone who is ambitious as well as kind. My friend Helen's mum once said: 'Getting married is the easiest thing a woman can do.' And I'm inclined to agree with her. It is easy to sleepwalk into a relationship with no personal standards because of fear that time is running out.

It is hard to build a life for yourself and invite someone in who you love and respect, who will treat you with the care and kindness you deserve. Instead of worrying that she isn't going to end up with someone, be thankful that your daughter hasn't settled for someone who isn't right for her. It sounds like she's a woman who wants as much from her partner and future co-parent as she has sought in every other part of her life. It sounds like you have raised a woman who likes herself. That's reason enough for a good night's sleep.

Sex

1. Dating

2. Friendship

3. Relationships

4. Family

5. Sex

6. Break-ups
   & Exes

7. Body & Soul

Dear Dolly: 'I am 19 years old and a virgin. What's wrong with me?'

I am 19 years old and in my first year at university. I am a virgin but desperately no longer want to be. Everyone else I know seems to have no issue getting railed, but for some reason it just hasn't happened for me. It's making me think there's something wrong with me. I don't think I'm particularly ugly or unsociable. However, I could really use some advice on how to get the job done, so to speak, because honestly the thought of being 20 and celibate terrifies me.

I don't personally manage the Dear Dolly inbox, so I often ask my editor for general weather reports from its varied climes. 'A lot of people in their twenties are worried about losing their virginity,' she informed me. I asked her to send me a selection of these emails – the agonizers ranged in age from their teens to early thirties; all of them were desperate to 'get the job done' and confused about why they hadn't already. Trust me when I tell you: there's nothing wrong with you and you're very much not alone.

There is no way I can respond to this problem without acknowledging the state of the world over the past two years. Recently a secondary school teacher friend told me her sixth formers had shared their concerns with her about going to university as virgins. I hadn't even thought of this as a ramification of Covid, but of course more teenagers are virgins. They missed all opportunities for virginity-losing between GCSEs and leaving school – house parties, 18th birthdays, school proms. Similar could be said of single people of any age – for parts of this year and last it was basically illegal to touch. I am 33 years old, and hope I can reassure you when I say that nearly everyone I know became a born-again virgin over the past two years. Even the people who live with a girlfriend or boyfriend.

I think it's also worth noting that you're moving out of adolescence and into adulthood in a time when sex is spoken about a lot. I think this is a good thing – the more we discuss and destigmatize sexuality the better. But I think one of the few downsides of the sex-positivity movement is that it can overstate the importance and omnipresence of sex. I know it feels like everyone else is getting railed all the time, but they probably aren't. And even if they are, their lives will not be wildly more pleasurable than yours. Most railing done at university is not the railing to be remembered on the deathbed.

But that's all too easy a thing for me to say now. When I read your email, among all the others, I was taken right back to the years when I thought I'd be wearing my virginity like a sandwich-board advertisement until the end of my days. Retrospectively I find it so strange that the simple act of penetration was The Great Quest for me and all my friends – the impossible task I dreamt of night after night. The way we talked about our virginities set up sexual experience as so phallocentric. We were never, say, excited about our first orgasms or the first time someone would kiss our naked bodies. I wish we had been as fixated on the discovery of our own pleasure as we were at the prospect of saying: 'I'm not a virgin any more.'

Spoiler alert: I did lose it in the end. As did all my friends. We ranged in age from mid-teens to early twenties. I would love to say I lost my virginity later than I'd wanted to because I was waiting for the right person. It wasn't that; I was horny as hell and I couldn't get a boy anywhere near me. When I did, it wasn't perfect but it was fun and so was he. I don't look back and wish I'd done it sooner. None of my friends now wish they'd done it sooner.

I would gradually learn this is how it feels when you finally get something you've always wanted: a job, a relationship, a flat. Once you have it, it becomes a part of your life and you adapt. A burden of yearning lifts and you don't really think about it any more. There are so many self-imposed milestones I set myself that have expired. By now I should have a driving licence and a baby and a life partner. I'm sure all those things are ahead of me if I want them. And I'm sure I won't wish for an alternative life in which they would have come sooner.

Like all these things, it will probably happen when you stop obsessing over it. When you're feeling relaxed and confident, and you meet someone nice who you get on with and makes you feel safe. Your virginity is nothing to be ashamed of, and it's also nobody's business but yours. Your future sex life will not be dictated by whether you lose your virginity at 19 or 20. You have a lifetime of shags ahead of you. And, I promise, they will only get better as you get older anyway.

Dear Dolly: 'I had sex with him almost immediately'

A nice man from a dating app offered to meet me for lunch. I slept with him almost immediately. How do I not act like a completely feral cat on the next date?

Sarah, 31

Well, hello Kitty!

First, I'd like to draw your attention to the specific language you chose for describing this romantic encounter. You say that he 'offered' to meet you for lunch, as if your profile on a dating app is a CV and this man an obliging employer. You also seem to be confessing that you slept with him on the first date, as if it were a shameful lapse in judgement. You then ask how to avoid seeming like a feral cat — unwanted, untamed, uncontrolled — simply because you had consensual sex with a fellow adult.

This leads me on to a larger observation, which is that you should ask yourself what you believe a successful date looks like and why you think you have messed up. It may be that first-date sex goes against your own personal values — you may like old-fashioned romance or the process of a prolonged seduction. You may have drunk more than you usually do on this date, which led

135

to an uncharacteristic shedding of inhibitions and garments. Or maybe it was because months of lockdown had finally got to you, and the thought of another night in with a Deliverooed yakisoba and the third rewatch of *Normal People* as you flailed around on your mattress was just too much to bear. If any of the above are true, then I understand why you feel disorientated by your decision to sleep with a near stranger.

There is another possibility I would like you to consider as the source of your worry. Do you believe that first-date sex is a mistake? Or do you believe first-date sex is shameful? I ask this as we are exactly the same age, and therefore we would have grown up on the same diet of cultural heteronormativity. On staples such as glossy women's magazines with cover lines like '75 tips to make sure your man is putty in your hands!' and 'Make him believe that moving in together was his idea!' Or the self-help books we found on our mum's shelves that explained why men love bitches or live on an entirely separate planet to us.

It is this literature I blame for the number of times I've known of women half-heartedly slurring, 'I'm very hard to get, you know,' in between feverish snogs in the corner of a dark bar, barely convincing themselves. For decades we've been told there are all these rules we have to follow in order to have a successful dating life: don't sleep with him on the first date; don't send the first text afterwards; don't seem too keen on the second date. But really, when you decode this language, all it means is:

be less. Less interested, less expressive, less open, less horny. The less 'you' you are, the more likely it is that he'll fall for you.

It is true that when you first get to know someone romantically, you cannot and should not bring all of yourself to a first date. Part of the pleasure of courtship is the slow unpeeling of a person. But abiding by a set of regulations that demand you ignore your instincts in order to trick someone into liking you is not only very boring, it's unfairly gendered. I can guarantee that this man has not spent any time since your last date worrying that he slept with you too soon, or that his desire for you might come across as wild and frightening when you next meet up. I doubt he has analysed the pros and cons of his decision at all.

If you think you would like a relationship with him, then obviously make sure you spend as much time getting to know him conversationally as you do physically. Or, if what you'd like is something casual, then it's fine to make it clear that you'd like to sleep with him again. In either case, please remember that you haven't failed at femininity by not withholding sex, when sex was exactly what you wanted. It's not embarrassing. It's not a sign that you caved too soon. You haven't lost any power-play game. These misogynistic myths of dating etiquette are constructed – they act in direct opposition to true connection and communication. And they don't mean anything. I don't know any half-decent men who would judge a woman for initiating sex on a first date.

And here's another idea: first-date sex might not be a

sign of future disaster, but rather a sign of chemistry. I know plenty of couples in long-term relationships that began with first-date sex. We must also acknowledge that you slept together after a *lunch*, which is incredibly French of the pair of you. I like to think you shared a Gauloise afterwards as you leant on the headboard in the late-afternoon light. I would spend less time fretting about this and more time boasting about it, quite frankly.

While I don't suggest you jump on this man as soon as you next see him, I ask that you do not think of yourself as a feral cat. Your sexual appetite does not make you needy, nor mangy, nor undiscerning. The fullness of your desire doesn't make you a desperate stray, rubbing up against anyone who will throw you any old kipper. You don't need someone to scoop you up in a carrier and take you home; you don't need a pleading advert on a pet adoption website asking for someone to choose you. You are, instead, a big cat. Exacting in your instincts, muscular in your moves, majestic in your prowl. Who knows what will happen? You may have found a fellow feline for a fling, you may have found the perfect partner in your pride. Either way, it sounds pretty fun.

Dear Dolly: 'I used to see an escort regularly and now I've fallen in love with her'

I used to see an escort regularly and now we have become friends to the point we spend nearly all our spare time together and I think I've fallen in love with her. We know each other's families and everything about each other. I did ask her to be my girlfriend a few months ago, but she rejected my suggestion and just wanted to remain friends. But the more time I spend with her, the more my feelings grow, and now I'm finding myself feeling things that I don't want to feel, like jealousy. She has been in two abusive relationships in the past and will not give up escorting. I know I should walk away, but then that would mean never seeing her again, which would probably be worse than knowing I could never be with her in a relationship. I'm so confused and it's starting to dominate every aspect of my life.

Steve

I struggle to think of few greater pains than being in love with someone who doesn't want to be with you. Recently I listened to a psychologist and expert on heartbreak speak of how it is a unique trauma, in that it is highly likely that the sufferer will go mad. A well-balanced adult who respects and cares for themselves can have their heart broken and instantly think and behave as if they are insane. Heartbreak often leads to an entire abandonment of self – we do things to stay close to the person we love, regardless of whether it is damaging for us. We spend time with them even if it hurts, and we obsess over them. It's completely understandable that this is dominating your thoughts, and I'm so, so sorry you're going through it.

I think you know what it is that you have to do, but I think you're not ready to do it. You'd rather stay in both pain and madness as a means to retain proximity to her than walk away from a situation that has no positive outcome. I get it – we've all been there. At one point or another we've visited a person's Instagram page so regularly over the course of a day that even when we sleep we dream in the squares of their grid. We've all pretended to be relaxed about something that pains us in order to continue to have someone in our lives. I can advise you all I like, but the truth is, only you will know when the need to preserve your heart and sanity has become greater than your desire to have her in your life.

Here is a simple truth you should remind yourself of – something that is difficult to confront, but will help you move forward. The fact she is an escort is not the reason you can't be with her – plenty of sex workers are in committed relationships. The fact she has been in abusive relationships is not the reason you can't be with her – lots of survivors of domestic abuse go on to be in healthy relationships. I'm sorry to say this plainly, but the obstacle standing in the way of a relationship with this woman is that she doesn't want to be in a relationship with you.

Which is no reflection of your eligibility – you're just not right for her. I also think it's complicated to enter into a truly equal relationship when the dynamic began as client and service provider. It's great that you managed to do it platonically, but she may not want to do it romantically. She probably has highly considered rules about relationships with former clients. Romance might feel like too great a leap.

But they always manage it in the movies! I know, I know. Richard Gere and Julia Roberts lived happily ever after in *Pretty Woman*. There was a romantic resolution in *The Girl Next Door*. There would have been a happy ending in *Moulin Rouge!* had there not been the tragic twist (Ewan McGregor's singing). But all these narratives worked on the premise that the female protagonist needed to be 'saved' from her job as a sex worker. I wonder if you believe that this woman needs rescuing, and the road to rescue is a relationship with you. What if she doesn't need a saviour? What if she wants to continue in her job or, in fact, enjoys her job? While your concern for her wellbeing is valid, it seems like it's not needed. Continuing to love her and feeling jealousy by doing so will not only be traumatic for you, it's unfairly shaming of her and her choices.

If you still find yourself unable to detach, ask yourself this: don't you want to be with someone who really wants to be with you? One of the symptoms of heartbreak-induced madness is that we convince ourselves that no other connection will be the same and we will never love anyone else. This is not true, and you'll only realize it once you make a clean break from the friendship and give yourself some time to heal. That process will probably take a while. But you will soon realize that while your love for this particular woman is unique, the magnitude of it is not. You can love again – just as enormously and wholeheartedly. But it can also be simpler; it can hurt less. At the risk of sounding sentimental, you're the person whose wellbeing you should be most concerned with right now. You're the only one with whom you know you have a long and certain future. That's a relationship to invest in – so save that guy instead.

Dear Dolly: 'How can I put the spark back into my relationship in my sixties?'

My partner and I have been together for ten years. We are both in our sixties (he is in his late sixties) and have great fun wining, dining, socializing and travelling. Sex was frequent, fun and sexy, often at least three times a week, but now we are lucky if we have sex once a week, frequently instigated by me. He has talked about erectile dysfunction and I do think he has issues about his age. However, I recently (unexpectedly) found him watching porn and there were clearly no issues there . . . I felt quite rejected because I am more than able and a willing partner. What can I do to ignite some spark back into our relationship?

Before I begin, I just want to ask everyone in a home county who is reading this with their breakfast to make sure they've chewed and swallowed whatever they're eating. I can't have you all choking on your toast – I don't want the blood of all of Berkshire on my hands. OK. Done? Great. Let's get going.

I understand why this might alarm you or feel like a rejection of you as his romantic partner, but I don't think it should. I don't think it's anything to do with you and I don't think it means your relationship is necessarily in trouble. Human sexuality is divided into two parts: the part that is for ourselves and the part that we share with another/others. Having a relationship with your own body is a positive thing – knowing what feels good and being able to do that without relying on someone else is great. Obviously the more our autonomous and collaborative sexuality join up, the better – nothing makes for more intimate sex than being able to invite someone into your private desires and fantasies. But I do think everyone, no matter what their age or marital status, has a right to a relationship with their own sexuality that may well remain private. It was there before he met you and it will be there if you ever left. I don't think that's an unusual thing. I would hope that you have a relationship with your own body and sexuality away from him too.

I'm cautious to say the following, because there is obviously no standard of 'normal' when it comes to sexual appetite, and I don't want you to feel any sort of shame for your libido (we love to see it, girl). But I do think having sex once a week after ten years of being together seems pretty good. If you're feeling unsatisfied, it's something worth addressing, but in terms of worrying about waning chemistry, I wouldn't let that frequency stress you out.

I would be amazed if erectile dysfunction and his age aren't the main factors behind him initiating sex less frequently. I remember once hearing a man who suffered from erectile dysfunction say in an interview that he felt like he was 'a romantic who couldn't make love' and I found it so sad. Changing bodies and subsequent difficulties with sex are obviously not just a male problem, but it must have a huge effect on a man's sense of self. Particularly if your relationship until this point has been as passionate as you describe. I'm sure he feels anxiety about not disappointing you or you seeing him as anything other than vital and virile. If that's the case, your reduced sex life isn't a reflection of your relationship, it shows a disconnection he's feeling from himself. That might not preclude his use of porn because he doesn't have an emotional relationship with the women on screen. He won't feel like he's letting them down if he can't 'perform'.

I don't want you to blame yourself in any way – it certainly isn't incumbent on you to find this elusive 'spark' and put it back into your relationship. I don't think that's the thing that's missing. What's missing is communication. If you talk to him about it and make him feel safe enough to open up to you, I'm sure you can find a way to restore your sex life to a place where you feel secure and satisfied. It might be as simple as him needing medical assistance. Or . . .

Everyone chew and swallow your toast again. All done? . . . you might have to more regularly find other ways of being intimate and physical than having penetrative sex. Or you could try watching porn together and finding something you both like, so he can invite you in on his sexual rituals and it can be something you enjoy mutually. (Although that might not be your thing, in which case ignore this suggestion. You should only do that if it's a thought that turns you on.)

Whatever the solution, you're only going to get there by talking. I know that might sound daunting or hideously uncomfortable, but I think you will feel such a relief after you have a conversation about where you're both at. It sounds like you two are a close and connected couple. If that's the case, you should make the most of being able to talk to each other about anything.

Dear Dolly: 'I'm seeing a married man, and the thought that I'm just sex to him makes me feel worthless'

I have been seeing a married man for eighteen months. I accept he loves his wife and children (who are the same age as me), and I am not asking for him to love me, but the thought that I am just sex to him makes me feel worthless. I don't want to lose a man who means so much to me, but it isn't fair that he gets to play happy families while I have to play the stoic other woman. How do I know when the time is right to end our relationship?

You're right that it's unfair. It's unfair that the man you love gets to enjoy the stability of a marriage and family as well as the excitement of a secret sexual relationship, while one woman is betrayed and the other is left feeling worthless. This hasn't happened by coincidence. There's a reason why so many affairs involve men in middle age and women in their twenties. I don't know if you are just sex to him – he may have very strong feelings for you. I do know that closeness to you probably makes him feel young and exciting and desired and important. One day you won't know him or love him any more and, as hard as it may be to imagine, you won't be sad. You'll just be really angry.

Reading your letter, the thing that I find most alarming is not that you're having a relationship with a married man, but that you seem to think you are so undeserving of love. We know that affairs rarely end well and can cause cataclysmic damage, the aftershock of which is often felt by multiple people. So why do so many do it? Particularly, in this case, when you're not 'asking for love'?

The old adage tells us that infidelity is not the problem in a marriage, but a sign that there are other things not working. I think something similar could be said of single people who choose to have affairs with married people. Attraction is, of course, an obvious motivation – but I would argue that the affair is a symptom that something is not working in the relationship you have with yourself. All of us fancy people we can't have all the time. It might be because they're in a relationship or we're in a relationship. But only some of us decide to act on it. It's far too simplistic to believe it's on account of a lack of morality, particularly because most people I know who have had long-term affairs are shocked from start to finish that they were capable of it.

Maybe you think you can't be loved the way other women are loved – fully, honestly and respectfully – so instead you settle for affection that is hidden and half-formed. When I interviewed the writer Marian Keyes, she said of the tumultuous relationships of her twenties: 'I was generating fake emotions to distract myself from the pain of being me.' I think about it all the time.

Perhaps you have embroiled yourself in something dramatic and maddening to avoid facing other issues. If that's the case, being properly single means you'll have to work through them, which I know is really scary, but it will set you free.

In terms of the right time to end the affair, you know the answer already. This is never going to be a relationship you're going to look back on and wish lasted longer. I hate saying this because I know it's going to sound judgemental – I really, really don't judge you – but it's important you know that this experience will stay with you. When you break up with him, you won't leave the affair in the past and never think about it again. I only know this from having multiple conversations with multiple women who had affairs with married men in their twenties. All of them, at some point in their thirties and forties, have been haunted by it.

You will think about it when you are in your next committed, long-term relationship. You will think about it at your best friend's wedding. You will think about it when your niece or goddaughter or daughter is your age. You will think about it when you are his wife's age. It's OK – every single one of us makes mistakes and all of us have regrets (I personally don't trust anyone without them, sorry Edith Piaf and Robbie Williams). But, in this moment of reflection, you have an opportunity to get out. There is a clear option for making life easier for your future self.

I can't be the person who gives you permission to

continue this affair or tells you that you have to end it. No one can, other than you. There's always a space between knowing exactly what you have to do and finding the strength and courage to do it. I think you're standing in that space right now. I hope you get to the other side soon. He can't come with you, but it's where you will find peace and integrity and truth. And love, if that's what you want.

Dear Dolly: 'My boyfriend of three years and I barely have sex'

I have been with my boyfriend for almost three years now and we barely have sex. I am 23 and he is 25 and his sex drive is so low. I try to spice things up, but when we do have sex it lasts for five minutes on a good day and he doesn't seem bothered about putting in the effort to please me. I ask him if it's me and he says it's nothing and that I want it all the time (once a week doesn't seem overly obsessed to me). We haven't had sex for a month now and I don't know how to bring it up without feeling guilty or like a sexual predator. I am planning on staying with him for a while, but if our sex life has already dried up that's a big, big issue for me. What would you do next?

My friend with a low sex drive once told me a story I've never forgotten. Her boyfriend, a very well-meaning man, used to have a pre-seduction technique that involved lighting incense and slathering himself in a thick layer of Nivea cream. She said the scent of the joss stick and the feel of his overly lubricated cheek ('like cold jelly') alerted her to the fact that she was meant to be horny. My friend with a high sex drive once told me a story I am similarly haunted by: during her countless unsuccessful goes at seducing her boyfriend over the course of countless months, he once reached for the excuse of urgently needing to descale the kettle.

It is horrible to feel pressure to have sex to please someone you love. And it is horrible to feel like you have to beg for sex from someone you love who doesn't want it. It is horrible for everyone. No one in your current situation is right or wrong – you are not a predator and he is not a prude. You are not a rampant pervert and he is not boring or complacent. The issue is that you are sexually incompatible. It happens! And it's a bummer. I'm really sorry.

My mum has a theory that every couple can be connected in three different ways: spiritually, intellectually and physically. She says you're lucky if you get two out of three, and I agree with her. One isn't enough for most people in the long run, and the rare three-out-of-three is an unparalleled miracle too overwhelming to sustain. (I've experienced it once. I'm glad I didn't end up with him because I think we would have locked ourselves in a house, gleefully flushed the keys down the loo and never left.)

What might be happening here is that you're not connecting physically. That one out of three isn't working for you both. What makes it complicated is that, while you may have the other two connections intact, the missing physical one is the one that is more important to you than to him. It is an absence that you can't ignore, and neither should you. Sexuality is so much more than how we connect to a partner: it can be how we connect to ourselves and explore who we are; it can be how we relax, release or subvert what it is we are in our non-sexual life; it can be a huge part of our identity. It's obviously important to you and you really, really shouldn't feel an ounce of shame about that.

It would be very easy for me to slip into the vernacular of 1980s glossy mags and give advice on how to *spice things up* (and, to be honest, I've waited twenty-plus columns to do so), but for everyone's sake I'll resist. For one, it sounds like you've already tried to speak to him about this with little success. Also, I think it's easy to overestimate the power of paraphernalia and tricks when it comes to a discrepancy in sex drives. A butt plug is just a butt plug – after all, it cannot change a person's libido. I could also start suggesting all sorts of theories about his sexual hang-ups or shame that might be inhibiting him, but that's probably overanalytical. Some people just aren't that sexually motivated, and that's fine.

But you both deserve to be in relationships where you feel entirely comfortable. You should free yourselves of these opposing pressures and by doing so avoid needless future resentment. I know it's easy for me to tell you to leave a relationship that I'm not in, and I know how painful and frustrating it will be to break up with someone with whom you are otherwise so compatible. But connected, safe, intimate, uninhibited sex with a like-minded partner is one of the best treats we get in the party bag of human experience. It's not something that should ever feel unavailable to us. But it especially shouldn't feel like that aged 23.

Dear Dolly: 'How long is too long to go without sex?'

How long is too long to go without sex? I came out of my marriage eight years ago and since then I can count on one hand the number of times I have had sex. I am nearly 47 and a good portion of my life has now become my 'celibate' phase, which may be self-imposed and all down to fear. I worry I have become completely sexless and will never do it again. I also worry that not having sexual confidence is part of the turn-off. I am not unattractive, but I really am scared of intimacy and rejection. Am I screwed?

There are many different reasons for celibacy and most of them fall into one of three categories: purposeful, circumstantial or accidental. The purposeful kind is the best and rarest – you can see its benefits in the eyes of its cheesecloth-wearing advocates. Or in the chapters of successful people's autobiographies in which they describe the most industrious years of their lives and simply state: 'I wasn't really dating during this time.' Circumstantial celibacy is less fun. Heartbreak, sadness, sickness, exhaustion, medication, children – these are all valid reasons for making sex a less urgent priority or shelving it altogether. Accidental abstinence – when you want to have sex, but you can't find the means to do it – is the real toughie. It sounds like you've experienced a mixture of these last two.

During various stages of lockdown in the past year, I've spoken to a lot of single people who have found themselves in a phase of accidental celibacy, which has sent them into despair. I've thought a lot about why this is, and I think it's because it reminds us of adolescence. For most people, enforced celibacy is one of the prevailing memories of teenage life – a frustrating combination of not having sex, but thinking about sex all the time. Obsessing over it, being terrified of it, googling the mechanics of it, wondering if we'd ever find anyone who wanted to do it with us. If you felt severely unattractive or rejected as a teenager, a long absence of sex in adult life can really agitate that old wound, no matter how much healing you've done in the interim. It can feel like you've regressed straight back into the (probably) lilac or lime-green walls of your childhood bedroom and returned to a state of inexperience and insecurity.

But you're not inexperienced. You're not underqualified. If you feel ready to have sex, you are ready to have sex. It might seem scary, but that's only because you're thinking of it as an abstract idea with an imaginary participant. The minute you connect with someone who you really fancy, intimacy won't feel like such a daunting thing. But you're not going to get there if you keep telling yourself you are sexless or that your lack of sex over the past eight years is in any way strange or a sign of failure.

Because there is no right answer to your question of how long is too long to go without sex. I know perfectly healthy people for whom a few days is too long. I know others who have happily not thought about sex in years. The amount you have sex says nothing about how desirable or sexual you are – it only shows your choices or circumstance. Sleeping with a handful of people in the first decade after a divorce is not as shocking as you think it is. Promiscuity can be an effective heartbreak prescription for some people, but it seems like you self-diagnosed that you aren't one of them. That shows you're someone who listens to their body (hot), has a solid sense of self (hot) and respects themselves (hot).

Also, don't get too hung up on this idea of being 'sexually confident'. What even is that? Yet another fake thing the Tomes of Heteronormativity have told us men want, along with being aloof (confuses them) and break-fast in bed (too much fuss). True sexual confidence does not mean being overtly horny, wildly kinky or a prolific shagger. Sexual confidence is knowing what you want from a partner and feeling unashamed to seek it out. It is understanding your own body and feeling comfortable in it. It is knowing that you deserve to feel really good. It is something you can find on your own and it has nothing to do with your tally of shags.

So no, you are not screwed, in either sense. But some great screwing awaits you, if that's what you're after. Your sexual self is not rusty or retired, it's not even on sabbatical. Your sexuality is right there, in your system and soul, right now. Alive and awake. You don't need someone to activate it for you and you never did. Only you get to choose when you share it with another person – you'll know when to do it and how to do it. And it will be really, really easy.

Break-ups & Exes

1. Dating

2. Friendship

3. Relationships

4. Family

5. Sex

6. Break-ups
   & Exes

7. Body & Soul

Dear Dolly: 'My boyfriend's lovely but I'm not happy. How do I end things?'

I've been in a relationship with my kind, loving boyfriend for nearly three years. I do love him, but I've known for a long time in my gut that I'm not happy. I often find myself dreaming of a different life. The problem is, I can't find the courage to end things. I've never broken up with someone before and I find myself worrying about what he would do, where he would live, how he'd tell his parents and what they'd think of me. I wish that we had become close friends instead of partners, and I hate the idea of losing him from my life. I feel paralysed with guilt and self-loathing. How do I fix this?

Ugh. The worst. I'm sorry. Some of the most distressing times in my life have been when I know I need to get out of a relationship and feel like I can't. I don't understand people who seem to do it so easily – I have always found being the heartbreaker rather than the heartbroken so much worse. Being heartbroken is intense and sharp and can make you feel like a wounded animal, but crucially there's somewhere to go with it. It's a pain with velocity. I find heartbreak is normally converted into something else, something productive or new. A life change, an epiphany, a greater strength, a mad haircut, a fling with someone born in the late nineties. Whereas the grief paired with the sense of responsibility that can come with ending a relationship is a dull but consistent pain. I still feel guilty about breaking up with someone a decade ago, someone who is very happily married with two children and I imagine never thinks about me at *all*.

The reason you're finding this so difficult is not because you're a bad person. Quite the opposite, it's because you're an empathetic person. Your instinct is to consider others and imagine what a feeling might be like for them – if you suspect it would be unpleasant, you want to do everything you can to protect them from that. That's a lovely quality to have, but it's not a very useful one when it comes to a situation like this. To state the obvious for a moment: relationships only function if you both want to be with each other. You can't people-please your way through being in love. You can't stay with someone because you don't want to have a sad conversation. Sad conversations are sometimes the only place where real life is waiting for us. And having them is the actual act of compassion, even if it doesn't feel like it. Truth is the most respectful thing you could give this man now, not cowardice disguised as kindness.

Here's a question someone asked me years ago that I now ask anyone who thinks they want to get out of a relationship: if you could press a big red button and it would all be over, would you do it? If you could find yourself out of this relationship and in a new life, but with no break-up chat, no division of assets, no exposure to their anguish, would you press it? If the answer is yes, you need to break up with that person now.

He might think he hates you for a bit. Or blame you. He might talk into a pint of lager for nights on end about how you ruined his life. 'He ruined my life,' is an old classic I love when I'm heartbroken. My favourite hit on the break-up jukebox – the tune my friends have to hear over and over again. The last time I was getting over someone, a very wise friend said to me gently: 'You know, no one should have the power to ruin your life by breaking up with you.' He was right, of course. If you're in a relationship where you think your entire purpose or self-esteem is dependent on the fact of the other person loving you for ever, something has gone wrong. My life was never their property to ruin, just as you should never feel like his is yours. And of all the men who I claimed once 'ruined my life' by not being with me, I would never reunite with any of them if given the chance. All the clichés are true about heartbreak: time heals, no one knows how long it's going to take, he will find a way to move on.

It will be horrific, then it will be sad, then it will be different, then you'll be free, and then you'll be happy. I am talking about both you and him. I try not to speak too emphatically in this column (blind leading etc.), but in this case it really does sound as though you need to break up with him. Now is the time to be brave and honest. He will find love again, just like you will, and both of you will be grateful that you made the decision to end a relationship that wasn't right. You are allowing him to find someone to be with who really wants to be with him. One day he'll know that was the real act of kindness.

Dear Dolly: 'My first love is now in a same-sex relationship and I can't stop thinking about it'

My first love was monumental, a decade-long on and off relationship — he was the most important kindred soul in my life. We ended it badly in our mid-twenties, and I have since been in a long-term and immensely happy relationship with my current boyfriend. A few years ago I found out my first love was in a relationship with a man, and they are still together now. I have always been a LGBTQ+ supporter, but it hurt me badly. Did he ever love me? Did he always feel this way? Didn't he think I would eventually find out and have these sorts of fears? When I am on my own they plague my mind, and I can't shake the overriding selfish thought: will I ever find relief from these questions without interfering with his new life?

Our emotions can be many things, but one thing they're not is rational. Fairness is not a tempering factor when it comes to raw feelings. Our actions should not be controlled by emotions, but they can be hard to talk down. Your feeling confused by your ex-boyfriend being in a relationship with a man is not a reflection on your support for the LGBTQ+ community.

Because, really, I don't think the fact that your ex is with a man is what's causing you to feel confused. And I don't know if what you're feeling is confusion. I think it's that your ex is with someone you deem your opposite, and this has made you feel inadequate. Even if he had ended up with a woman, there's a likelihood you would have focused on your differences to analyse your past with him. You look at his current relationship as a commentary on your time together, and you see his new choice of partner as evidence of what he found lacking in you.

Here is the boring truth – something that the fog of your feelings may not let you see yet: your ex's current relationship does not take anything away from the relationship you had with him. He did not go looking for a new relationship with the single aim of finding a different version of you or someone who would correct what you did or didn't give him. He didn't go on dates hoping to upgrade you. He fell in love with someone. And it has nothing to do with you.

I think the loss of a relationship and all the stuff we build within it – the language, the sex, the memories – is so traumatizing, we cannot let ourselves believe it disappears. We have to know it goes somewhere else. Perhaps this is why we imagine our ex transfers all that stuff straight on to their new partner, which is what makes imagining their new life so painful. But he's not reliving your relationship with a different cast member. He's building a new world with someone else. One where they have different language, different sex and make brand-new memories. He loves his boyfriend in an entirely different way to how he loved you – the two relationships exist separately, and he exists separately within them. You speak of how happy you are with your current boyfriend, but you also seem to have been very happy for the decade you were with your ex. Both relationships were the right one at different points in your life. I'm sure this is exactly how he feels about you too.

There are loads of possible stories of his sexuality. He may have always known he was attracted to men, but didn't tell anyone. He may have never known until after you broke up. He might not want to categorize himself at all. The only thing you know for certain is that he fell in love with two individuals who happen to be of different genders. Can you make your peace with this fact? Or do you still feel you need to speak to him? I would think carefully before you do: make sure you are opening a conversation in which he can share his experience, rather than you demanding answers from him. Both of your current relationships are none of each other's business. And he doesn't owe it to you to be with women for the rest of his life to satisfy your version of who he is.

If these thoughts still plague you, it doesn't mean it's because there is proof that he never loved you. The most solid proof of what you two had is in your memories. Hold on to these. They are sacred and they are not lying to you.

Recently, a friend of mine received a long message of

explanation from a man she had been waiting to hear from for years and years. She received it, screenshotted it and sent it to me, then deleted it without reply, her heart beating at a glacial pace. Her long-rehearsed speech, the one we've been rewriting in pubs since our twenties, came to nothing. She had always thought she needed answers to get closure, but she had done it on her own without realizing. The peace you're looking for is probably within reach.

Dear Dolly: 'I can't stop stalking my ex on social media'

I broke up with my ex just over a year ago and I can't stop stalking him on social media. He got Instagram shortly before we broke up and has recently started posting stories. Naturally I assumed he began doing this to get my attention. I also stalk his (and his friends') Facebook/Spotify/Strava . . . you name it, regularly! I find myself getting upset or making things up based on what I find. For example, I have convinced myself he's seeing a new girl purely because he and his best mate newly follow her on Instagram. How do I stop this ridiculous behaviour?

I once had a break-up and in the extremely tearful debrief we had a few months later I admitted to my ex that I hadn't been able to stop checking his Instagram and Twitter. He told me he had managed to only 'cave' a handful of times since we had parted. I asked him how he had exercised such self-restraint. 'There is nothing I could find on your profiles that's going to make me feel good,' he said. His logic infuriated me. I realized that it wasn't that he had more self-restraint than I did, he had more self-compassion. I was envious of it.

There is nothing you could find on an ex's profile

that's going to make you feel good. And yet the maso-
chistic treat of having a quick snoop can become an
addiction. Even the best-case scenario makes you feel
terrible: the heart-fluttering high of typing their familiar
handle into your phone, the suspense as the page loads,
the short, sharp relief when you find nothing of interest, the shame that you're back here again, the deleting
of the browser history so you won't do it again, the inevitable return to your old habit a few days later.

And, in the worst-case scenario, there is a small triumph in your pain – when you find morsels of public
information that confirm your most private theories: he
has moved on, he's with someone else, he doesn't care
about me, he never cared about me, I was right all along,
ha. Even though, as any seasoned millennial knows by
now, you can never be sure of the reality of someone's
life from their social media pages. You're never going to
know truly how your boyfriend is doing by creating a
forensic profile of guesswork based on comments and
posts and follows.

You need to stop this addictive cycle and you obviously cannot do it on your own. There's something that
can help you. The block button. Don't mute him, don't
'limit your social media usage'. It won't work. You need
to block. The first time I blocked an ex, I had such new-
found empathy for anyone who had blocked me. I used
to think it was because they hated me, or they were
posting things they didn't want me to see. It was only
when I blocked someone I still loved that I realized:

when someone blocks you it's not because they're worried about you going on their profile, it's because they're going on your profile too much. In the majority of cases blocking isn't a weapon used to make people feel bad, it's an armour to guard oneself.

I reluctantly return to the wisdom of the ex: there's nothing you could find on his profile that's going to make you feel good. Well. That's a lie. He could post a photo of himself looking particularly unattractive, maybe with a bit of sauce on his face, hopefully sobbing. The caption would read: 'Hey guys. Time for some real talk. Since my last break-up I've done nothing but think about her. I've tried to sleep with someone new, but the sex was terrible in comparison. I miss her every day. My family and friends aren't speaking to me because they think it's so stupid that we broke up, they're like, "YOU'RE NEVER GOING TO LOVE ANYONE THE WAY YOU LOVED HER. ARE YOU STUPID OR SOMETHING??!!" Anyway. I've cried myself to sleep every night, and even the dark escape of sleep isn't a comfort because every night I dream about her. Hope you're all having great weekends x.'

I have been waiting for this post from all of my exes and I'm sorry to say it won't ever materialize.

OK, the hard bit: he's free to do whatever he wants now. He's going to have sex with someone else, he's going to fall in love, he might get married one day. The likelihood is that is going to happen. And you don't know when.

It might be slowly over the course of the next fifty years, or it might be in the next five months. But the one guarantee is that his life is going to continue without you. You can't keep him on an invisible leash through knowing everything that's happening for him – you can't control anything hereon in. His life is all up for grabs.

But the good news is: so is yours. You're both free now. Block him, break the habit of stalking, then, by the time all his news gets back to you, you will have moved on. It won't feel like news at all.

Dear Dolly: 'I've been happily married for years, but I can't get over my first love'

I'm happily married (I think I am) to a wonderful man. My choices, desires and dreams are as important as his are, and he has often pushed me to go get them. Everything and everyone tells me how lucky I am to have this special man with whom I have been sharing my life for so long, but — and it's a very big but — I can't seem to let go of my past.

Many years ago I obsessed over a man who was my first proper love at first sight but who clearly wasn't keen on me. We got back in touch a few years ago on a WhatsApp group, and it's like I'm back at square one. After all these years, I feel the same way as I did back then.

I have kind of pushed him away again with my overzealous messages and he hasn't replied to me in more than a year. But I can't stop thinking about him. I feel so guilty and bad, because this isn't going to lead me anywhere, I know. Have you got any remedy, suggestions, anything? Please help me, I'm really losing it. I have never felt like this before. I hope you have solutions to this dilemma. Please help.

AT

One of the best pieces of advice I have ever been given is that when you're trying to get over someone, you need to focus on the facts of who they are rather than the idea of who they are. When it comes to desire, perception rather than reality is, more often than not, what fuels the furnace – what they represent to us, what we've imagined them to be, what we think they'll provide in our lives that is currently missing, who we think we'll be when we're with them. These imaginings can become an obsession, and the more we think about them, the harder it is to delineate between our self-created myths of a person and cold, hard facts. I am not diminishing your current pain and confusion but I do think it will help if you can differentiate between the story that currently exists between you and this man and the story you've penned in your head.

From the timeline you've given me, it appears that you're in your early to mid-forties. While that is a young age, it does mark the beginning of the middle of your life. You have entered the second half, which I imagine could be exciting and invigorating or disheartening and draining, or all of these things (much like a night at the National Theatre). Far be it from me to speculate on a crisis, but you might be fixating on a man from your past so you don't have to think about your future. Not to put too fine a point on it, this obsession might be less about him and more about a fear of ageing.

I have heard it said that the further away we get from our first love, the more we ruminate on it. Why is that?

First love is so rarely the greatest love – the sex is clumsy, we don't know who we are when we're so young, we often miscommunicate, the lust can be overwhelming, the break-up can feel like a death sentence. I think the romance of first love increases as we grow older because we miss the freedom we felt in those relationships. There was no pressure to commit, no bills to pay, no children to raise, no sense of what lies ahead, no cynicism about what could go wrong because we were too young to know what something going really wrong feels like. Perhaps what you're craving is not a relationship with this man but to once again be the teenage girl who was struck by her first *coup de foudre* while standing in the student union bar, pint of Boddingtons in her hand.

But if you were to be with him now, neither of you would be the students with whom you're trying to reconnect. You cannot time travel back into your past for longer than an hour or a night. You've known and seen and felt too many things to fully rehouse the mind of your teenage self. If you're trying to beat the laws of physics, it's not going to work.

It also strikes me as no coincidence that you've been with your partner a number of years now, presumably with a milestone anniversary somewhere on the horizon. Maybe you are worrying about the familiarity of your long-term relationship – that you've fallen into a routine or that things have become too predictable. I think that's entirely understandable. It's also no coincidence that the man you've chosen to focus your passion on is one whom you describe as having little interest in you and who you don't seem to know hugely well. Unrequited obsession over a relative stranger – you couldn't have chosen something more dangerous or more unfamiliar.

You need to go cold turkey to get some clarity. No messages, no daydreaming, no social media stalking. Warning: it will feel like drug withdrawal. That doesn't mean he is your one true love, it is chemicals leaving your body. But you need to give yourself some space and time to think about what you're really looking for every time you turn to this fantasy. What gives you relief or escapism – is it a sense of excitement? Romance? Promise of new adventures ahead? Because these are all things that can be achieved in other ways than walking out of a functioning, happy relationship in which you share a rich history and certain future. It is hard to do, perhaps the biggest challenge of loving someone across a lifetime, but it isn't impossible.

A final word of advice: whatever you do, do not watch the TV programme *Normal People* on BBC iPlayer.

Dear Dolly: 'I'm worried that the sex I had with my ex is the best I'll ever have'

I love sex. I love having sex, I love talking about sex. Some of it has been great, most of it has been fairly average and a lot of it has been awful. However, the physical connection that I had with my ex-boyfriend was, and I say this with the full acceptance of cliché, mind-blowing. We would have sex four or five times a night every time we saw each other — even after more than a year together. I have never felt anything like it. Unfortunately for many other reasons the relationship didn't work out. I'm now starting to get back out there but the few experiences I've had have been pretty underwhelming. I am so worried that I will never experience that same level of sex again. What if he's the best sex I will ever have?

In every new relationship where the sex is particularly great, it is hard to imagine a world in which that insatiability won't last for ever. Every couple in the thrall of a particularly horny honeymoon phase (which I think can last for anything up to two years) secretly thinks they've hacked the rule of long-term monogamy that tells us that sexual energy will, at some point, wane. We have images of ourselves, decades in, still staying up until dawn four times a week on account of a shagathon. Becoming parents together and having a giggly quickie in the public loo at Legoland. Being randy pensioners stealthily going at it in a golf buggy.

And yet so few of us manage to sustain that intensity, no matter how good the sex or how much we continue to fancy one another. For most people that urgency for sex – that sense that you might die unless you cut your night out short and get in an Uber to their front door RIGHT NOW – diminishes and something else replaces it. Something more relaxed and responsive to the relationship's phases. The first thing I'll say to try to put your mind at ease is that, while I am sure your sexual connection would have continued to be incredibly strong, the likelihood is that it wouldn't have remained as full-on as it had been. A relationship involves two humans, two bodies, two brains, two lives – to sustain such an unwavering sex life while moving through life and its cycles would have been almost impossible.

And if you had continued having that much sex, that seems more like a compulsion than a connection. An addiction to a sexual partner can be fun but it's not healthy or sustainable in a relationship, and I'm sure you want sex to be a joy rather than a dependence. Also, I don't know if five back-to-back shags in a night would satisfy you in the long term. Hear me out: I think part of the fun of relationship sex is that you form a sexual catalogue together over a period of years: the sleepy sex you have when you both wake up in the middle of the night and then forget about until one of you mentions it the following day; the ferocious renaissance f*** after a fortnight of no sex; the sudden sex on the sofa that surprises you both while you're watching *The Crown*. That variation makes those moments of intensity feel incredibly real. Plus, if you're at it *all* the time, you'll clear your local Boots out of Cystopurin, which isn't fair on the other women who live in your area.

I would be cautious of a relationship in which sex is the most important and honest form of communication. Sex is important in a relationship, of course it is, but if you are reliant on it to connect with each other without much else, I think it can give a false sense of closeness that will ultimately fall apart.

And I'd also warn against thinking in superlatives. Something I've learnt from living for a few decades is that the superlative you refer to won't be the superlative of a lifetime. Life is long and unpredictable and so much is ahead. The year that I thought was the worst year of my life turned out not to be the worst year of my life. The day that I always said was the happiest was topped by another day. I thought I'd met the man I was most in love with until I eventually fell in love with someone else. The best sex of your life is definitely not a thing of the past, and I'd try not to spend too much time on such a fatalistic thought when the future is so unknown.

Be glad that you had such a wonderful sexual connection with someone. Say thanks (to the universe, not to him, definitively don't send a text of thanks to him) and think of it as a soupçon for the future. Your ex wasn't a sexual superhero – the sex you had was something you did together. Good sex is about fancying each other, being communicative and open. That will happen again with the right person.

Dear Dolly: 'Can I be friends with my ex?'

Can you really be friends with an ex? I came out of a seven-year relationship last year. He was the best friend I ever had. We are each now in a new relationship and are trying hard to remain friends. We see each other once a week, but I am worried that as our respective relationships become more serious we will lose each other. It feels very painful not being the most important person in his life any more, a dynamic that intensifies as his new relationship progresses. Do I let him go now and cut him out until it is less fresh? Is it possible for us to remain in each other's lives in any meaningful way?

I've always been envious of couples who manage to stay friends after they break up. I find it exceedingly chic. It's so rare for two people to put their egos aside, let go of resentments and manage respectfully to devolve a romantic connection into a platonic one. I know some exes-turned-mates who say that friendship is exactly where they were destined, they just had to go through coupledom to get there. I know others who say they're so close as friends, they can't even remember what their sexual and romantic connection was like. I even know an actual, real-life pair of exes who became godparents to each other's respective children. Just like Hugh Grant and Liz Hurley, but without the sex scandal.

I think most people have at least one ex they wish they had found a way to stay friends with – a person they instinctively want to call with good news or bad news, or when reminded of an old in-joke. Ten years on and there is still an ex-boyfriend I want to call when I hear certain albums or visit certain places. This type of ex can live in your mind almost as much as the other kind – the one you only ever want to see named on an obituary page.

It's rare for exes to become long-term best friends, and with good reason. Even if you do manage to do it – successfully divide the assets, not hold grudges, not get drunk and have a nostalgia shag – even then, that's only half the work done. You then have to explain this friendship to your respective partners and make them feel comfortable with it. In my experience that's the thing that is the biggest obstacle to long-term friendship with an ex.

I don't think it's unreasonable that someone's current partner might not be thrilled by their boyfriend or girl-friend having weekly meet-ups with a person who they were with for seven years. And I don't think that dis-comfort is because of jealousy or feeling threatened that there might still be a chance they will get back together.

I think it's about occupation of intimate space. If you're someone's long-term partner, you are meant to be the person who sees them the most, knows them the best and is familiar with every part of their life. This will be an impossible role for your ex's current girlfriend or future girlfriend to fill if you are still in his life so regularly. How can she quickly catch up on the seven years you spent with him? How can she get as close to his friends and family and find out everything about him?

It's telling that the thing you're most worried about is 'not being the most important person in his life any more'. I wonder if that's the thing you're grieving, rather than a potential friendship with him. You can still see him and stay in each other's lives in a more casual way that leaves some room for new love for both of you. But maybe you're worried about fully letting go of the relationship you had together.

The fact is: he wasn't your best friend for the past seven years, he was your boyfriend. So once you strip him of that job title and its requirements, once you are no longer the person he wakes up and goes to sleep with, your relationship is going to be less intense. It has to be.

I think you need to say goodbye to your old relationship. This could be with an honest conversation with your ex in which you work out the new boundaries and a looser schedule of your friendship. Or it might be work you have to do on your own. This might be with the help of a therapist, talking with mates, a lot of thinking or even with a witchy ritual in which you cut romantic ties with him. (*I'll see you in the crystal shop by the sage sticks!*)

It will be hard initially. You could feel the full force of delayed grief for a relationship you never mourned because you've been on a watered-down version of it while you both wean off each other. But you haven't lost him. And you will be the most important person in someone's life again – you'll be each other's ally, teammate and other half. But you're not going to be able to experience or commit to it if your ex is still the most important person in your life.

Dear Dolly: 'I've gone through a break-up that feels like I have had my heart ripped out. The pain is too much to bear'

I've gone through a break-up that feels like I have had my heart and all other organs ripped out of me and stuffed back in. I'm 22 and this is my third heartbreak, but my biggest for sure. I know that heartbreak depends on the length of the relationship and the amount it meant to you, but does it get easier? Do you have any wisdom to impart? This is the first time I have felt pain that is too much to bear.

When I was studying journalism I was taught by a woman called Marcelle d'Argy Smith. She was editor of *Cosmopolitan* in the 1980s and is a sage on love and relationships. In our first lecture she told us of when she once visited a friend who had just been diagnosed with a terminal illness. 'How do you feel?' she asked. 'It's not as bad as heartbreak,' her friend replied.

The most devastating thing I've learnt in my thirties so far is that heartbreak doesn't get easier. I'm sorry not to be able to deliver more hopeful news. I can't believe it either. But it turns out it doesn't matter how much therapy you've done. It doesn't matter how many friends you've watched make mistakes or how many agony advice columns you've read (waste of time).

Our capacity to be humiliated and humbled by love is evergreen, and there's something wild and extraordinary about that. It is a part of us that never ages and it corresponds through every stage of life: the teenager who was dumped, the woman signing her divorce papers.

Recently I saw a friend who turned 50 this year, a single mother with three grown-up daughters. Every time we speak she has another story of a hot night with one of many interchangeable lovers. Whenever I ask if these nights could lead to something more, she always laughs and tells me that period of her life is over – she has learnt to have fun with men without getting attached. This time, however, she told me she had just promised a man she had met a month ago that they were boyfriend and girlfriend. 'You're not going to believe it,' she said. 'I'm madly in love.' It is a beautiful, terrifying fact: just as our vulnerability to heartbreak never changes, neither does our vulnerability to fall in love.

The only thing that gets easier is that you know heartbreak ends eventually. The more it happens, the more certain you are that you'll be fine. You can't put an exact timeframe on it and it's never like the films. You won't find yourself in a 'getting over it' montage in which you become a new woman while an Alanis Morissette song plays. But one day you'll wake up and your ex won't be the first thing you think about. You'll have a dreamless sleep in which their face is absent. You'll notice early-morning light spilling in from your bedroom blind and you'll remember the fun that came before them – fun that is sure to come again. Heartbreak is like internal gridlock: for a while there's nowhere to move in a traffic jam of thoughts. Then a tiny bit of space frees up without you realizing and you can finally feel something else.

Until then you need to distract yourself as much as possible. And when distraction won't do its job – when you're crying on the Tube as you listen to that *bloody* Lana Del Rey album – know that you're processing something. You might feel like you're wasting weeks of your life in meaningless pain, but you're not. You're moving through it. You're getting closer to the other side.

I once had my heart broken – a proper sledgehammer job – and I went for a drink with a friend who is happily married in her forties with a child. My tears collected in a wine glass and I told her that I wanted to sleep until it was over. She held me by the shoulders and said: 'One day you'll look back on this and you will think, I was never more alive.'

I don't want to romanticize your pain, but I now understand exactly what she meant. Grief is an electric shock that tells us we are fully alive – it means we're connecting and creating and caring. We're participating. We're making the most of this short go. We're opening up and taking risks, we're tangling ourselves in other lives.

Next time you feel one of those further cracks of heartbreak, think of it as a strange sort of privilege. The magnitude of your loss reflects the magnitude of your love. You will not feel like this for ever, I promise, and what will be left is awe that you could love someone so much. You're experiencing something that will soften and harden you, give you strength and allow you to be weak. You loved someone and it changed you. Aren't we the lucky ones.

Body & Soul

1. Dating
2. Friendship
3. Relationships
4. Family
5. Sex
6. Break-ups
   & Exes
7. Body & Soul

Dear Dolly: 'I am 19 years old and have no confidence when it comes to my appearance'

I am 19 years old and have no confidence when it comes to my physical appearance. I am extremely outgoing, I am good at making friends and I am happy with my life at university, but I just can't shake the feeling that I often feel like the ugliest girl in the room. I think the worst part is knowing that it's mostly in my head but still being unable to feel any different. I can't bear to be in photographs and I can't leave the house without make-up on. I also have never had a boyfriend, and although I know you will say there is an abundance of time for that in the future, I sometimes look at my beautiful best friend, who is about to go into her third serious(ish) relationship, and wonder if things would be different for me if I felt validated romantically. Can you offer me some wisdom on how to care less about looking beautiful?

First things first: being concerned about your appearance shouldn't make you feel ashamed. I hear you – it's frustrating and grim. There's not one woman alive, currently doing her Sunday-morning chin pluck or barefooted weigh-in, who doesn't wish she didn't care. But of course we care – we exist in a society that has told us, from the day we were born, that how we look is our most valuable commodity. It's hard enough to process this without scolding ourselves for being shallow or anti-feminist because we don't jump out of bed, grab our tummies and dance around merrily as though we're in a Special K advert.

The definition of beauty is never as prescriptive as when you're a teenager. When I was 19, the word 'beautiful' was a synonym for 'Sienna Miller'. We did everything we could to look like her (and many of us still have the fringed moccasin boots to prove it). One of the many perks of getting older is that we develop individual style as we understand our own faces and bodies better. In turn, we all start getting horny for people who look nothing like our teenage crushes. It is, and I can't stress this enough, an absolute joy. Hotness quickly diversifies as you enter adulthood. Body hair, greying hair, baldness, scarred skin, piercings, freckles – these are just some of the things that you will find yourself fancying as part of the whole package of a fit human. A series of relationships does not 'prove' attractiveness – but please know that there are lots of people who you've never met, who you can't even imagine, who are going to be very attracted to you.

There are antidotes to low self-esteem, and changing the way you look is the least effective of all of them. Anyone who has hated themselves and tried to fix it with an extreme diet or an expensive dress will tell you the same thing: the thoughts remain. They might quieten for a while, but they return – editing the surface only acts as a short-term fix. The true transformation of self-esteem, the 'you-won't-*believe*-the-before-and-after' makeover, does not come from perfecting appearance. It comes from forming character.

You can do this by being a loving and thoughtful friend. Or being really funny. Becoming obsessed with something, losing yourself in it passionately and knowing everything about your chosen subject. Being helpful to strangers when no one is there to see. Leaving relationships when they no longer make you happy. Campaigning for a cause you care about. Being able to laugh at yourself. Developing a work ethic that you can be proud of. Keeping yourself safe and healthy. Ambition. Curiosity. Knowing what you like in sex. Knowing how to change a light bulb, fuse or tyre. Saving spiders instead of swatting them. Any of these things will help. These very small, very unexciting steps are what build a sense of integrity and self-respect. They help make the mirror reflection feel a little less important. And the best part is, character is far more robust than appearance. Many variables can affect how we look – it's so much harder to be robbed of your character.

You will one day wish you could take back the time that self-hatred is currently occupying. Of all the people who have mistreated me over the years – who have said the cruellest, most inhibiting things – the one I most wish I could speak to is my younger self. I wish 19-year-old me could have somehow received a letter from me now. So, imagine that you in ten years' time is sending you a message. Imagine her telegramming it through me, because I know what she wants to say. She wants me to tell you that you'll never be as young as you are right now – that there are so many potential ways for you to leave an impression on the world. She wants you to realize all of them. She says you should enjoy the vitality and freedom of being 19. She's looking at a photo of you now and, I promise, she thinks you look perfect.

Dear Dolly: 'My girlfriend has given up drinking and now judges me whenever I have a beer'

I love my girlfriend, but I feel like we see 'fun' in different ways. My social groups are quite centred around alcohol – not over the top, but we certainly enjoy multiple drinks at the weekend. My girlfriend used to drink but has stopped over the past few months, which is obviously fine by me, but I feel like she has begun to judge my alcohol habits by starting fights if I come back a little half-cut or commenting if I have a beer to relax. I really don't want to see her as boring or not enjoy her company because of her change of habits, but it's starting to bother me. What do I do?

OK, so before I launch into my response, let it be known that I am broadly on your side. I think a lot of people can have alcohol in their life in a functional way – for relaxation, celebration and escape. And that doesn't necessarily mean always being moderate. I think that healthy alcohol use can allow for excess – sometimes the sensation of excess is the very point of drinking. As long as everyone is happy, as long as the nights of excess don't happen excessively, I think it's cool. I am responding to your letter in good faith and believing you when you say that your drinking is recreational and harmless, rather than destructive or something you're powerless to resist, and in which case, yes, this is an overreaction from your girlfriend. But there are loads of possibilities for why she's responding like this that go beyond her being annoying or trying to spoil your fun. Increasingly I am realizing that the function of an agony aunt (other than being woefully sanctimonious towards strangers) is to empathize with the person the agonizer is writing about and imagine their point of view. So that's what I'm going to do.

You speak of the irritation you feel about her new sobriety and perceived piousness, but say little about her journey to sobriety. Why did your girlfriend stop drinking? Have you talked to her about it? Is it that drinking has a detrimental effect on her mental or physical health? Is it that she didn't like how she behaved when she drank? Is she worried about her lack of control when it comes to drinking? Is she close with someone who has addiction problems? While none of these is a valid reason to judge your drinking habits or demand you stop drinking, they are important for the context of her seemingly reproachful comments. Perhaps you are focusing on her sobriety as a judgement on you, rather than taking an interest in why she has made this choice.

Home is the place where we are meant to feel safest and most comfortable. Maybe being in the presence of alcohol or anything associated with it makes her feel anxious. If that's the case, I don't think it's unreasonable that you be sensitive to that. While she's still adjusting to sobriety, you could do your boozing outside the home and with people other than her. There is, however, a possibility that this isn't a short-term adjustment phase and that she now wants an entirely alcohol-free life and partner. I don't think there is anything wrong with that, but I also don't think that should be required of you if alcohol is something that brings you great pleasure. It sounds like it's an important part of your social life and how you unwind – I don't think you should feel ashamed about that.

The only thing I worry about is your implication that you now find her boring. Is that because you think she is being judgemental? (Judgemental people are very boring.) Or is it because you find her sobriety boring? If it's the latter, then either you are too dependent on alcohol or your relationship was too dependent on alcohol. You should be able to have fun together without getting pissed – you should still be able to find enjoyment in each other's company, ease in conversation and things to do together at the weekend without booze. If you're feeling the absence of drink in your shared time, maybe you need to try doing things that don't remind you of alcohol. I'm not going to list suggested activities because there's nothing less horny than a list of activities and I don't want to make it seem like your new sober life with your girlfriend has to be like a Butlin's schedule. But the point is, you can still have fun together. It just might not be the kind of fun you were used to.

As always, it's just going to be easier if you talk to her honestly (there's that 'does what it says on the tin' sanctimony!). Her judgement is probably coming from a place of self-protection or fear, and it will be so much easier to navigate if you understand it a little better. If you love her it's definitely worth working on. And if she is reasonable she will see that you can support her sobriety while also continuing to enjoy a personal relationship with alcohol. From one boozy Suzy to another – I hope you work it out.

Dear Dolly: 'I'm a lesbian but I can't stop seeking the approval of men'

I'm 99.9 per cent sure I'm a lesbian but I can't stop seeking the approval of men. There's a guy at work who I find quite repulsive but I know fancies me and I can't stop leaning into it. It's like I'm too scared to tell everyone at work I'm gay because I don't know how to exist without being a viable option for male attention. How do I shake the need to be fancied by all men at all times when I know I have no desire for them?

If you were to read the majority of my WhatsApp conversations with women, what you would find is a series of confessions that are slight variations on your question. Admissions of heterosexual guilt, secret fears that we aren't as good a feminist as we believed we were, realizations that some of our unexamined thoughts are so disappointingly patriarchal. 'I think I want an engagement ring', 'I miss the pervy security guard at work', 'Max Mosley: fit?'

I think part of the cognitive 'work' of being a feminist, whatever a person's gender, is to look at our instinctive thoughts about the world and humanity and reflect on how those thoughts got into our minds. Were they inherited from the previous generation? Indoctrinated by culture? Implanted by authority? Which of them do we agree with, and which ones contradict our beliefs? Which ones do we want to keep and which ones do we want to question? That is how an authentic belief system is formed, and it's important that we're willing for it to be constantly evolving.

But I also think part of the work of being human is to forgive ourselves when we realize that we were conditioned to think things we eventually learn to be wrong. I once read someone say that there are no such things as bad thoughts, only bad actions. I found this a liberating way to think and live. You're experiencing a dissonance between how you want to behave around men and your impulses for their attention – that's OK. What's important is that you want to change. Your question comes across as clear-eyed and self-reflective, which is already much more work than most of us do on ourselves.

I wonder if your workplace is a particularly misogynistic or macho one. I was very lucky in that my first office job was creative and in a super low-key and liberal environment. Other friends of mine went straight into the corporate world, and when we would come together to talk about work I'd realize how different our office experiences were. Some of the girls had to comply to a formal office dress code, a lot of them were in the minority in meetings and conferences, all of them, at some point, felt patronized or diminished or leered at by their male colleagues. Perhaps a fresh start in a new workplace would help make you feel more at ease and like you can be yourself. No one should feel obliged to disclose their sexuality at work, but they also should never, ever feel like they have to hide it.

I also wonder whether your friendship group is majority straight or whether you have a community of gay friends. If you're constantly around heterosexual people (along with the default in culture still being so woefully heterosexual) that may be exacerbating your instinct to seek approval from straight men. Maybe spending more time in queer spaces will help quash this urge to stand in the eyeline of the male gaze. You may meet other lesbian women who are fighting a similar internal battle to you and you can talk, or maybe even just laugh, about it together.

The best way to unlearn these learnt beliefs and behaviours is through self-education. That might mean reading feminist literature or listening to feminist podcasts, but it also might be through discussion. I think you need to find some like-minded women who are on a similar journey of growth to you and have a similar keenness to think. Perhaps you could seek out a feminist book group or an online community that hash out these subjects together in a safe and sensitive environment. Learning that other women have worked through similar self-contradictions (which, I swear to you, they have) might act as a huge relief. And, crucially, it could help you change the direction of those long-held thoughts.

I also think you should take it easy on yourself. Humans are full of inconsistencies or even hypocrisies and examining it all is a lifetime's work. And while it is so admirable that you are aware of the discrepancies in your own identity, you also mustn't feel a pressure to politicize every thought that you have and chastise yourself for it. I am sure there are days when even the most well-read, clued-up, right-on woman enjoys a wink from a cheeky bus driver or a compliment from a male colleague. There's enough shame loaded on women from birth without us loading even more on ourselves for not being a good enough feminist. All that is important is that you don't feel disempowered at work. And that you feel safe to be who you are.

Dear Dolly: 'I want to help my best friend with her eating disorder, but I am still struggling with my own'

My best friend recently opened up to me about her eating disorder. I want to be the most supportive friend I can be, however I have been struggling with an eating disorder myself for many years. (She is aware of this, which, I'm guessing, is why she came to me.) I find that when she talks to me about her problem, it triggers me. This makes me feel so guilty and like a bad friend for not being able to help her. Should I accept the friendship will perhaps be detrimental to my own recovery, or should I just distance myself completely? I don't want to hurt anyone.

I am so sorry for what you've been through. And I have huge respect for the amount of thought you are giving to how to support your best friend while also taking care of yourself. You are not a bad friend. You're clearly a person who shows compassion to themselves and others, and she is lucky to have you.

It makes total sense that your friend speaking about her eating disorder has made you feel distressed or anxious or potentially vulnerable to relapse. You have been through something traumatic and are in the process of recovery, which is a delicate and deeply personal experience. Hearing someone talk about the details of their eating disorder – even using particular words – can instantly transport you back into memories that feel very frightening. It doesn't matter how much she loves you or you love her or how good both of your intentions are, it's just how trauma works.

I think what people sometimes struggle to understand is that recovery, for many sufferers, is a lifetime's work. Even when someone is living an ostensibly happy and healthy life, it's rare that the thoughts have dissolved entirely. We always have to be sensitive about how we speak about food and exercise to those recovering from eating disorders, in the same way that we should be sensitive about alcohol when we're in the company of a recovering alcoholic. You can never truly know the internal battles that someone in recovery continues to fight. It's easy to forget – I'm certainly regretful of how I've forgotten it myself. I imagine she feels very lost and sees you as someone inspiring and full of wisdom, which is why she chose to confide in you.

It's really encouraging that she has opened up. As you will already know, another thing that people often don't understand about eating disorders is that no one hates talking about eating disorders more than the person who is suffering from one. It's a living hell, it's incredibly private and it can feel hugely embarrassing. You are right to acknowledge that her new openness with you should be handled sensitively.

I think it's really important, for you and for her, to

have an honest conversation as soon as possible. Tell her that you love her, but that the stage you are at in your recovery means you can't be exposed to the details of her eating disorder. Tell her that you appreciate how much she trusted you to talk about it. You can word it without sounding accusatory – prepare some thoughts before you have the conversation. Share any resources that have helped you: support groups, charities or counselling. If those particular things haven't been a part of your recovery, then maybe you could do some light online research (they're easy to find) as a suggestion.

You can also help her find a different safe space for her to discuss her eating disorder. Chat about who else in her life would be supportive and trustworthy while also able to receive her experiences. Together you can work out a suitable and reliable confidant.

I once heard Brené Brown talk about a study on empathy. The researcher examined highly empathetic people to find out what they had in common. There was one uniting factor: rock-solid boundaries. These were people who knew how to protect themselves. They knew when to say no. They preserved their emotional energy so that they were able to pour as much genuine love and patience in the places where they could be most useful. Hearing this was such an important lesson for me. People-pleasers are often liars – they keep everyone else happy at their own expense. They can end up resenting those they try to serve, and thieve themselves of their own compassion reserves.

'Boundaries' is one of those self-help words that is often misused or overused. Having boundaries doesn't mean being self-absorbed, it means being truthful about what you can comfortably give. It means self-preservation and self-respect. It means deep intimacy with the people you love, because you're being honest with each other. In order to be the best friend you can be, you have to keep yourself safe. You can support her and make her feel loved without entering into discussions about her eating disorder. You must never, ever feel guilty about making your recovery the number-one priority. I hope you're doing OK. I'm sending all my love to you.

Dear Dolly: 'I get biblically slaughtered every time I get drunk'

As a member of the unfortunate graduating class of 2020, I have decided to forgo the job search in favour of moving to Paris for a year. I'll be working as an au pair, trying to improve my French, and hopefully meeting the cynical, Breton-striped Gallic provocateur I've always dreamt of. The thing is, my friends have long joked that my life goal is to be French, but I have a long history of getting biblically slaughtered every time I get drunk. I never mean to, but I have a terrible tolerance. From what I understand, the French are very dismissive of British drinking culture (obviously also the British in general), so how do I manage to enjoy a glass of wine at a streetside café without inevitably making a tit of myself? Any help with faking French sophistication much appreciated.

I think it was Marcel Proust who wrote: 'It is rarer to meet a man with three bollocks than a twenty-something English woman who doesn't describe herself as "a Francophile".' How reassuring it is to know that we have all once slept with wet hair because we read that Caroline de Maigret said it's how she achieves her natural wave. How spectacularly predictable of us to have thought we were the first woman to have a highly specific fantasy about Serge Gainsbourg. How adorable of us to have begun a new year with 'Resolution one: take a lover' written in our notebooks, and ended it with a handful of failed Hinge dates with estate agents. We have all, at some point, gone into the hairdresser's for an Amélie bob and come out looking like Chairman Mao; clutched a photo of Jean Seberg on arrival and emerged as Just William. You are not the first girl to fall foul of a Primark Breton T-shirt and a Truffaut film poster, *ma chérie*, and neither will you be the last.

What is it about Frenchness that we long for so passionately? What about Frenchness makes our Englishness feel so mortifying? I think the first thing is their understatement. Coco Chanel told women to take one thing off before they left the house; we are the island of the beaded shawl and American tan hosiery. The French know the beauty of moderation – of having a sliver of cheese with a baguette, one cigarette with a coffee, or allowing children a small glass of wine at dinner – we, on the other hand, are the proud home of the snakebite and a battered saveloy.

I suspect the other most-coveted facet of Frenchness is their apparent fearlessness. We are a nation preoccupied with manners, given to awkwardness and worried what everyone thinks of us, whereas it is made out that to be French is to give fewer f***s. They, apparently, don't make small talk about traffic and weather and are unafraid to engage in political debate. They shrug instead of grin. They sleep with whomever they like. They eat dinner after 9 p.m. and have an enviably cavalier attitude to indigestion.

All that being said, I really don't think the French disapprove of us nearly as much as we think they do – that's a very old-fashioned way of looking at the dialogue between our cultures. And it's probably a suspicion inherited from our parents, who learnt about France from watching *'Allo 'Allo!* and reading *A Year in Provence*. I am sure you don't need me to tell you that the oaf:sophisticate ratio of the French population is probably about the same as ours. To generalize an entire country's temperament is to close yourself off to experiences and encounters before you've even got there.

I can think of few things more embarrassing than an English person in Paris overidentifying as French. So, before you board the Eurostar, it might be useful to break down exactly what it is you are looking for from the next year. Think about your Parisian idealization and figure out the specific qualities to which you aspire – the answer won't be simply 'being French', but something else that exposes your self-doubts.

I wouldn't worry about the drinking. I've always been a great champion and defender of drunkenness. Being consistently measured has become such a virtue, and I'm not sure if it's for our own happiness or our own megalomania. Some people thrive on moderation, but it's doesn't work for everyone. Some of us need a touch of extremity. You don't seem to be regretful about how you behave when you're drunk, it seems like you're worried what French people will think of your drunkenness. As long as you're staying safe and not hurting anyone, I don't see the problem with sometimes drinking too much. I worry about modern puritanism wiping out the next generation of great lushes and roués. And while I'm not suggesting you should mount the bar of Café de Flore in a pearly button-studded jacket and sing 'Knees Up Mother Brown', I do think you'll get the most out of this trip by being yourself.

And you will have to be yourself, I'm afraid. Yourself will find you, whether you're applying red lipstick in a Montmartre café or browsing for books you will never read in Shakespeare and Company. Here's the thing we all learn at some point or another: you have to take yourself abroad. You can go on an adventure (for which I applaud you, everyone talks about going to Paris for their moveable feast, you're 21 and you're actually doing it), you can meet new people, you can learn new things about the world and yourself. But all your anxieties and quirks will follow you across the Channel, so do not expect a city alone to make you a different person. You can take a holiday from your postcode, but not your DNA. Approach the next year with lightness and openness, rather than with an expectation of a full personality transformation.

And if Paris fails you? Well. We will always have Primark.

Dear Dolly: 'After a five-year relationship, I'm incapable of being single'

I am a 23-year-old woman who six months ago came out of a five-year relationship. After a short mourning period I've spent the past few months jumping from fling to fling, using dating apps to have a handful of micro relationships with men, only for them to fizzle out and for me to be left feeling empty. When these flings end I feel an almost unstoppable urge to get straight back on the apps and find another one, and the cycle repeats. I am incapable of being single. The thought of spending Sundays on my own fills me with dread, and even though I've been seeing loads more of my friends since the end of my long-term relationship, I still feel lonely and miss sharing my life with someone.

You're not incapable of being single. I haven't had the experience of exiting a five-year relationship, but I have lots of friends who have, and all of them have followed this exact pattern: they cry for a week, then they join a dating app for the first time and feel like they've come out of a coma; like they briefly touched death and have been resurrected. They start obsessively chatting to a handful of people, and when you see them they order an excess of tequila-based cocktails and say things like: 'I want to be single for ever!' They go on their first date, they get on well, have OK sex, then immediately try to make that person their partner. It doesn't work, they cry again, they go on another date and the same thing happens. This goes on for about a year until one of their dates relents and goes out with them. Or they decide to commit to single life.

It makes sense that you're craving a romantic partner. It is all your mind and body has known for your entire adult life. But wanting something because it's familiar doesn't necessarily mean it's right for us. There's a phrase my therapist says to me that I will pass on in this column free of charge (because what is therapy if not a way of repurposing another person's clinical training as your own wisdom): 'What got you here won't get you there.' In other words, being in a long-term relationship was right for you until six months ago. But now it feels like you want a different experience for this next phase of your life.

Now I've got to be careful here because I know I can get a bit *Eat Pray Love*-y on the subject of spending time alone. And I don't want to unduly romanticize long-term singledom, because it's not for everyone and it does have its challenges. It's not all solo holidays and people-watching in cafés, and perhaps I have overstated this in my writing in the past. (A woman once said to me that her friend was inspired by my memoir to live on her own 'surrounded by books and plants'. 'She doesn't even read,' she muttered.)

But what I will say is this: in my late twenties I decided to learn how to be on my own. I'd been a lifelong commitment-dodger and I decided to finally commit to myself. It was the best decision I ever made. I used to be obsessed with romantic love and, like you, couldn't imagine how life would be stimulating without it. I have since gone not months but whole years without dating. In the years that I haven't spent with a boyfriend, inheriting his habits and taste, I have fully come to understand my own. I know exactly how I like to spend my weekend (Friday party, Saturday dinner, Sunday cinema), what I always need in my cupboard (cornichons, Tabasco, French mustard) and what time I like to go to bed (11.45 p.m., with a ten-minute allowance to browse my saved searches on the eBay app).

There are so many parts of myself that fill me with doubt and loathing – my intellect, my appearance, my knowledge of any history (*why do they name centuries weirdly?*). But my independence brings me an enormous sense of pride. To feel like you can be with yourself – that you can keep yourself safe and be at peace in your own company – I now believe is the greatest and quietest confidence a human can know.

Allow me a little whimsical bullshit to finish: the key is to externalize your spirit. Think of her as a friend or a twin sister. A girl you've known your whole life who is going to be with you until your last day on Earth. You do share your life with someone. She is your company for ever. Listen to her, nourish her, challenge her. Learn together. Be in conversation with her always – remove her from situations when she is unhappy and lean into pleasure when that is what she wants. You will fall in love again and experience romantic partnership. And then maybe again. Then maybe again and again. And those relationships will be so much better when you know you are choosing, rather than need, to be in them. Learn to be with yourself now. Your future self will thank you.

Acknowledgements

First and foremost, I want to thank everyone who has ever written in to Dear Dolly. The column and this book could not exist if it wasn't for the stories that are entrusted to me by strangers. I am so grateful for your vulnerability and honesty when writing to me.

Thank you Helen Garnons-Williams for your support, editing and curation skills and your patience – I have loved working together. Thank you to Juliet Annan for telling me that this book was a good idea – as usual, you are right about everything. Thank you to my friend and agent Clare Conville for all of the hard work you give my career, and all of the support you give me.

Thank you Surian Fletcher-Jones and China Moo-Young, my collaborators and mentors, for helping me problem-solve in scripts, on set and in my personal life too.

Thank you Alison Williams and Roisin Kelly for all the help with putting this collection together. Thank you to each of my editors at the *Sunday Times Style* – Jackie Annesley, Lorraine Candy and Laura Atkinson. I am so thankful for the opportunities you've given me and everything you've taught me. I still can't believe I get to write for my favourite magazine.

And thank you to my best female friends – for the advice, the wine, the pints, the vodka, the voice notes, the

Zooms, the weeks away, nights at the table and days on the sofa. You help me figure everything out. I don't know how I would have got through the last few years without you.

Bonus Columns

Dear Dolly: 'My boyfriend won't add me on social media'

Pre-lockdown I had started seeing a lovely man who was much nicer than any man I've ever dated. Kind, funny, fit and fantastic in bed. As we were only two months into dating when lockdown happened, I thought it best if we stayed separate, hoping that absence would make the heart grow fonder. It did in terms of our phone contact, but he resolutely refused to add me on social media. He said we already spoke every day and there was nothing else to know, but I find it strange, like he has got something to hide. I know it sounds like such a small matter in the grand scheme of things, but it really bothered me. I felt like a dirty little secret, and what started off as a joke ended with him rolling his eyes and saying, 'That's what my ex said.' We ended up splitting as, aside from this, I grew increasingly upset at the fact he didn't want to commit. However, we have recently been in touch and are meeting next week when I am back in the UK. What do you think, Doll? Even if he now wants to commit, is the social media thing still a bit weird?

Dm-ming and ah-ing, Stockwell

I have thought about this for three days and I have decided it is weird.

There are a number of factors that could make it less weird. If, for example, you described him as the sort of person who doesn't really understand the omnipresence and significance of social media. The sort of person who calls someone's Instagram profile their 'website', who does Zoom calls with only half their forehead present and whose email address ends with @btopenworld. org. I could perhaps then understand why he couldn't grasp why actively denying someone access to your social media profiles might feel suspicious.

It would also be a bit less weird if you had both decided not to follow each other. I know a few couples who made a joint decision to date and get to know each other at the beginning only through real-life conversation and experience, rather than trawling through Facebook holiday albums from 2006 titled 'Girls Just Wanna Have Sun'. I even know a couple who decided not to follow each other on social media until the day after their first child was born, which they liked to show off about. I put this couple in the same category of people who have never owned a television or claim to have never eaten a McDonald's, and I have absolutely no interest in spending time with them.

But the thing that makes this indisputably weird to me is when you pair it with the fact that he has been commitment-avoidant. Also I am not reassured by the fact that he spoke to you every day during lockdown – people who are commitment-avoidant in real life are often hugely committed on WhatsApp. It is where they can try out the fun of being in a relationship without any of the work. The men who message you 500 times a day are more often than not the ones who will never describe a relationship as more than 'just hanging out'.

I don't think you're his dirty secret and I really would be amazed if he has anything to hide. There is so rarely anything worth hiding on anyone's social media profiles, apart from the people who do those Instagram videos in which they unpack their shopping bags and explain every item they've bought. Or share their haikus on modern life. I wish they'd hide those. I don't think this is about him wanting to keep you out of public sight and I don't think he has a dual virtual life – I think this is about him exercising control over you.

A classic commitment-phobe is someone who doesn't let their romantic partner have access to their full self, whether it's not introducing them to their friends or family, not bringing them back to their home or not opening up to them about their past or their vulnerabilities. It is a way that they, often subconsciously, can hold someone at arm's length, so they don't have to immerse themselves in the mortifying and beautiful experience of intimacy. It's not that they are ashamed of who they are, they just think if they keep who they are partially concealed then they can stay slightly disconnected from the relationship. This could be for a number of reasons. They might not want a relationship. They might not be ready for the trust and surrender it takes to be fully known. They might have been very hurt in the past and are terrified of this happening again.

I think this is a man who likes to keep the woman he is dating at a bit of a distance. You should be simultaneously comforted and alarmed by the fact that he also did this to his ex and she also found it disorientating. If you have the strength and energy to be patient and magnanimous, then ask him why this is such a problem for him and make him feel safe enough to articulate the real reasons for his resistance. You say he is the nicest man you've ever dated, so you should trust your instincts if you think that this could be a relationship worth fighting for. It might be that this is truly just a personality quirk that is rooted in some semblance of logic or past pain.

But I also don't think you should stay with someone a bit rubbish in the hope that they will once again become the lovely person you first met. This is the tried-and-tested method of pick-up artists: give her the performance of being Mr Perfect in the first flush, then she'll spend the rest of the relationship holding out for his return.

The shorter answer to all of the above is, of course, to date a person who isn't on social media at all. I've heard they exist.

Dear Dolly: 'My boyfriend's man-child habits really annoy me'

I love my boyfriend, but his man-child habits are really starting to grate on me. He lives off pizza from Sainsbury's, his room is a tip and on a weekend away he brought his luggage in a plastic carrier bag. We've been together for ten months and he's never cooked me a meal.

Despite this, he is kind, caring, thoughtful and emotionally intelligent, and we love each other so much. We're both in our early twenties. Are all straight men like this at our age? Or does it get better? We've spoken about this stuff before, but nothing seems to have changed. I can't expect a man to change for me, right? But sometimes I wish he was a little bit 'wholesome'.

With love,

A girl who's getting a bit fed up

I am going to be straight with you – this is an issue that never fully goes away. I speak to you from the beyond. A decade from where you stand, I can report that friends of mine are still ending up at a date's flat for the first time and finding no sheets on the bed. I know women who send their mother-in-law a birthday card and sign it on behalf of their son. I know women who have to threaten divorce to make their husband clean the bathroom. When some of these marriages break down and those men finally find themselves on their own, I am certain they will perish prematurely and the coroner's report will state: 'Flame Grilled Steak McCoy's'.

Which is not to say that women can't be slobs too. I also know of women who get their five-a-day from a packet of Skittles and whose bedsheets are tie-dyed with fake tan. The crucial difference is they normally don't expect a man to organize their life for them, because you would never find a man with the patience or inclination to do so. Those women are perpetually single, cigarette ash flowing out of jewellery boxes, vibrator always kicking around their bed like a scatter cushion, not burdening another person with their infantile chaos.

Before I go on, I think it's important I note that I don't think there is anything necessarily wrong with being a slob. Some people are more than happy living in mess, having no routine and being badly organized. I think that's fine. I also think it's fine to do this for a short period in your early twenties, when everything already feels like such a mess. You might as well commit to the theme. There is a certain type of grubby glamour to be found in those initial years of flat-sharing. My friends and I regularly talk about the fact we lived in a house with a downstairs loo that didn't work for more than three years, for no other reason than we couldn't be bothered to call a plumber. It was easier for us to create a glittery door sign that said 'LOO NOT WORKING' as a speech bubble coming out of a photo of Anthea Turner's face than it was to ring a plumber.

However, living like this does become a problem if it's making the person unhappy, or those who love them unhappy. Is it stopping him from being the best version of himself? Do you think that he would find things easier if he bought a holdall for a weekend away instead of using a plastic carrier bag? Or – a more difficult question – are these things that you want on his behalf? Does he even want a holdall? Do you want him to have a holdall because you'd like to know you're the sort of woman who is with a man self-respecting enough to own luggage?

Because – and I really don't want to seem like a Sainsbury's-pizza apologist – if he's merrily kicking his way through his early twenties as a bit of a disaster, I'm not sure you should try to change him. Not only because it is something he may grow out of, but also because it's not very fun for you to make a labour-intensive project of your partner, a relationship that is meant to be a place of mutual compromise and acceptance.

The plain fact is this relationship will self-expire if nothing changes. Your irritation about his man-child ways will soon stop being merely annoying and will instead become deeply unsexy. If self-reliance and self-care are things you need in a boyfriend (both completely valid desires), then you will find it increasingly hard to respect someone who cannot do these things. And the minute you lose respect for someone, you'll stop fancying them.

I am wary of making too many generalizations about men in their twenties and how childlike they can be, but I do think my friend had a point when she said: 'A man will only meet you at the place where you lift the bar.' I think it might be an idea to really spell out to him how much his habits are frustrating you and pose a threat to your relationship. If you really love him, it feels fair to give him a chance to change himself, rather than you trying to change him yourself.

But also you don't want to be in a relationship where you have to constantly explain to him how to be a boyfriend. And you don't want to be in a relationship where you always feel like a parent and you're never served a similar sort of care. If you know that he is not going to change and it's really going to bother you, then break up. The grimmest truth I have from the beyond is, sadly, there will nearly always be a woman who is willing to look after a man like your boyfriend. Messy girls get punished, messy boys rarely do – there is a reason 'woman-child' has not yet found its way into casual parlance. So you can always leave that job to someone else and stick to the work that gives you a pay cheque.

Dear Dolly: 'My mum calls me ten times a day. It's too much'

How many times a day can my mum phone me? I'm 26 and her only child. We used to talk once a day, maybe twice, but since my dad left her three years ago it has risen to seven to ten times and accumulates to an hour on the phone with her every day. I've just moved in with my boyfriend and work in finance, so free time is important. I often try to not pick up/only pick up every other call, but then I get shouted at for not answering before. I've tried to tell her not to ring me first thing as neither I nor my boyfriend needs another alarm clock. She also expects me to be able to chat when I'm in the office. I love her but it's draining, especially as I get berated during every call too. How do I manage her?

Oof. Seven to ten times a day. That's a lot. The only person who has ever contacted me that much is the Labour Party and I'm sorry to say I had to unsubscribe from its mailing list. In response to your first question of how many times can your mum call you a day, the answer is limitless, depending on her personality, your relationship with her and what she's going through. I am extremely lucky, in that I have a hands-off family when it comes to phone contact. My family's WhatsApp group

227

is populated with casual check-ins, boomer-friendly anti-government-themed memes and messages my mum sends to her entire WhatsApp contact list when they were only meant for her sister (most recently, her Amazon wish list and a knitting pattern).

But some of my friends aren't as fortunate and a part of their daily life is managing their mother's need for near-constant communication. In almost all these cases there has been a really unpleasant implosion when the pressure has become too much for the daughter and she finally snaps. One of my friends didn't speak to her mum for nearly a year in the wake of one of these arguments because her mum was so hurt by the revelation that her daughter felt harassed by her. I think it would be really kind and really grown-up of you to have conversations with your mum now to stop that from happening further down the line.

If you're writing to me for an outside opinion on whether your mum's demand for your time is unreasonable, my thought is: yes. It is. No one should be asking for that much of you unless they need one-off or urgent care. And, more broadly, I believe that a sense of personal freedom is a fundamental part of daily contentment and I resent anyone who keeps someone glued to their phone against their will. Some people's love language might be constant messages and calls, but for the people from whom they're demanding this level of communication it might make them feel claustrophobic or, in your case, like they can't do their job or live their life.

First things first – you have to have a conversation with your mum in which you tell her that you can't keep up this level of communication. Be very sensitive with your wording – it seems like your mum's compulsion to chat is because of loneliness or a fear of feeling alone. She obviously likes being involved in your life as it makes her feel needed and a part of a community. Tell her how lucky you are to have such a loving mother who is so available and communicative but you need to find a way to have regular check-ins with each other that also allows you to be present in other parts of your life.

Then you need to draw up some boundaries. I have seen through my friends who speak to their mums a lot that routine is really helpful. Find a time in the week that suits you both and have a rule that you don't speak for longer than you're able to give. For example, is there a walk you do to a station or bus stop for work every morning or evening? Could that be your mum time? Or maybe it's twice a week while she's cooking her dinner? Only you can work out how much time you can feasibly give to her and when, but I think regularity and routine will help things feel less relentless and out of your control.

Finally, I think you should suggest spending less time on the phone and more time in person together. Get out your diaries and plan some days over the next six months. Go and stay with her, go on a night away together if possible, book the theatre or cinema, go for a long walk together. Make it clear to her that you want to spend quality time with her, where she has your full attention, rather than distracted time on the phone.

I know you must feel incredibly guilty, but remember: your mum had her chance to forge a young adult life independent of her mother. It's only right and fair that you get the same.

GOOD MATERIAL

DOLLY ALDERTON

From the bestselling author of *Ghosts* and *Everything I Know About Love*

Andy's story wasn't meant to turn out this way. Living out of a suitcase in his best friends' spare room, waiting for his career as a stand-up comedian to finally take off, he struggles to process the life-ruining end of his relationship with the only woman he's ever truly loved.

As he tries to solve the seemingly unsolvable mystery of his broken relationship, he contends with career catastrophe, social media paranoia, a rapidly dwindling friendship group and the growing suspicion that, at 35, he really should have figured this all out by now.

Andy has a lot to learn, not least his ex-girlfriend's side of the story.

Warm, wise, funny and achingly relatable, Dolly Alderton's highly anticipated second novel is about the mystery of what draws us together – and pulls us apart – the pain of really growing up, and the stories we tell about our lives.

'An absolute knock-out . . . Alderton's voice feels like your very favourite friend'

Taylor Jenkins-Reid, praise for *Ghosts*

'Utter BRILLIANCE. Dolly is such an insightful commentator on love, longing, friendship and emotional landscapes'

Marian Keyes, praise for *Ghosts*

'I loved it – Alderton has clearly mastered every form of writing, which is a surprise to nobody'

Candice Carty-Williams, praise for *Ghosts*

Available to pre-order now

Publishing in hardback, e-book and audiobook 02/11/2023

WWW.PENGUIN.CO.UK